How to write travel articles ...in one weekend

By Diana Cambridge

GW00802087

Published by Canal Street Publishing Ltd.
1 Coburg Villas, Camden Road, Bath, Somerset, BA1 5JF.
www.canalstreet.org.uk
First published in Great Britain in 2007.

Designer: Richard Gale
Resource listings: Julie Venis

A catalogue record for this book is available from The British Library.

ISBN 978 - 0 - 9553391 - 1 - 0

Printed and bound by HSW Print
Tel. 01443 441100

How to write travel articles ...in one weekend

Contents

Hello,

You'd love to have a travel article published – or you wouldn't have bought this book! And there are so many travel-related topics now – your weekend trip to a European capital, your place in the sun, holiday food and wine, activity breaks, even a local journey that's familiar to you, yet "travel" to a stranger – they're all there, ready to write about.

Writing about all these can add so much to your travel experience – packing a notebook, looking forward to the trip, imagining the piece you'll write when you get home and seeing it in print with your name on it. That's every writers' dream!

Yet how often do we actually get down to writing about our travels? All too frequently, we lose confidence along the way; we feel too self-conscious even to make notes or we become blocked by the feeling that other writers are much better than we are – so it isn't really worth even trying, is it?

But believe me, it is! And this weekend I can show you that you needn't be held back in your travel writing by feelings of self-doubt. You have what it takes to write a travel article. I can give you the confidence you need, the practical know-how, the tricks of the trade... all in 48 hours in your own home. As someone who once found travel writing the most daunting challenge – even though I desperately wanted to do it – I know exactly how you feel. And I can help.

I can show you that you can write about any journey and turn it into a travel article. I give you ways of capturing ideas and framing them into written outlines. Your saleable journeys needn't be expensive to take – your local bus ride tomorrow could be a magazine feature in three months time, with your name on it. It's all a question of ideas, angles, honesty, confidence to write and sending out your work – and that's what I'll give you.

If you read my first book, *How to write magazine articles... in one weekend* (Canal Street Publishing Ltd., £9.99), you'll know how strongly I believe in coaching, and in setting goals. I can be your coach this weekend, and with my tips you'll also have tools to coach yourself and to set the essential goals for your writing. But none of it is arduous or complicated – this will be a pleasant and relaxing weekend for you, even with ideas for interesting foods and drinks which will sustain you.

At the end of this 48 hours – which could be in any part of the week, if your weekends are not free – you will have completed one travel article, and have a few ideas for your next. You'll be surprised how much you'll have learned about the basics of travel journalism. And you'll be elated by the writing plans you can make!

I'll be at your side all the way. We'll reach the completion of your article together. But it's up to you to send it off! And with the new confidence I'll give you, I know you will…

Diana

1 – Getting started

'I think some of the best modern writing comes now from travellers.'

~ Michael Palin

Welcome to your weekend course in travel writing! These 48 hours could be your best – and most profitable – ever. Because at the end of it you – yes, you – will have completed a travel article and sent it to a magazine editor. That's your goal for this weekend – and you will achieve it.

Travel is exhilarating, it's easier than ever before, and it renews and inspires us. And writing about travel can be just as uplifting. You want to keep a record of what you do and see, you want to write and you'd love to see your work published. So far, so good!

But when you sit down to write a travel piece, maybe you're sabotaged by negative feelings. *What shall I write? I'm not good enough! How can I dare to be a travel writer when there are so many famous ones out there?* You wonder whether you could really be a travel writer. Perhaps you feel you lack experience and authority, and the confidence to write with conviction. How can you possibly write about places in a way that will compel readers to want to visit them? How can you write in a way that will inform and entertain readers? You may think it calls for a skill you haven't got! You may simply feel that your writing isn't "good enough". But many professional writers suffer from this lack of confidence – and I've noticed that travel writing seems to create much more anxiety than other forms of journalism.

People feel they have to be something special to write about travel, something they're certain they're not. But they're wrong. You are special. All you need is conviction about your writing – and about yourself. This weekend, I can without doubt give you the confidence you need to get your travel article written, polished and sent off to a magazine.

Work your way through the ten sections of my book. Think of them as chunks of a weekend course – a course you don't have to drive to, or read your work aloud at, or worry about whether you'll be able to get to sleep in a strange bedroom. Each section will move you on, and step by step my Ten Golden Rules, one at the end of each chapter, will ease you into completing a travel article – this weekend.

Travel writing is just you offering readers your unique slant on a place – with tips, suggestions and advice that you might offer to a friend who is a new-comer to the country, city, area or even village you're writing about. It's just writing, and since I believe travel writing needs to be personal, maybe you're offering a little insight into yourself as well.

How I started – and learned

The thought that travel writing called for extra-special qualities – and that I didn't have them – was my big obstacle when I wrote my first travel pieces. I was confident enough in my abilities as a newspaper journalist – I'd been one for ten years – but was hard for me to believe that I could tackle travel. At the back of my mind, I felt you had to be "better" to write travel – cleverer, seriously well travelled, and generally more accomplished. Was that me? I didn't think so.

All of those doubts made my first piece, for a woman's magazine, nowhere near as good as it could have been. It was about Gwent in South Wales, where I lived. I packed in far too much detail, and didn't let my personality come through. I was too hesitant and nervous to write with vitality. Instead, I concentrated on description and facts that made for an acceptable feature, but not a brilliant one. I was so traumatized by the task that I didn't start it until the last possible minute, and then it took me hours to write!

But the next piece I did was different. It was much stronger. It was about Paris, where I'd spent three months as a mature but not very wealthy stu-dent. I focused on getting around Paris on a budget, on unusual places to see and go that didn't cost much – the clairvoyant in the basement of a smart department store, the free guided tour of the city's sewers, the cheap books of Metro tickets you can buy, the pavement stalls selling delicious crepes with fresh orange and lemon sauce for a couple of euros – or francs as they were in those days.

The Paris feature was accepted by several women's magazines, and maga-zines for ex-pats and business travellers. I knew then why my first attempt was almost a flop, and why the Paris feature flew. I discovered that as well as facts, travel pieces need personality. All I need have done when writing about Gwent was to put the emphasis on my favourite spots and list my per-sonal bests: shops, restaurants, interesting cafes, churches, parks and museums. I could have found a 'landmark' date; an anniversary that would have given the feature a topical angle. I could have zoomed in on one particular aspect of Gwent rather than trying to cover the entire county. I could have freed up my creativity. I could have shared something of myself.

Since then, I've written and had published travel pieces about Bath, Bristol, Brighton, Newcastle upon Tyne, Edinburgh, New York, South Carolina, Majorca, Venice and many parts of Greece; I even edit a monthly glossy magazine that's just about Greece. When I see my magazine in WH Smith, I'm so proud of it, and of my team of freelance writers who make it so special.

As an editor, I get my best travel pieces not from trained, professionally qualified newspaper or magazine journalists, but from very gifted amateurs. Some of them are people who have retired from careers – as teachers, civil servants, secretaries; others are still working, in jobs ranging from health therapist to travel agent. Professionally unqualified they maybe, but they can write many trained journalists off the page.

I've experienced travel writing from every angle – a freelance selling work, an editor commissioning and buying work from freelances, and as a publisher trying to cut costs and increase subscriptions – that's the commercial element of my job as an editor. But one of the most exciting parts of my work is talking to readers who want to write, and to new freelances. I try to encourage them to boost their confidence, to release their creativity, and not be hemmed in by the idea that travel writing is "special".

And that's what I can do for you, this weekend. So let's start!

7 goals!

Over this weekend I want you to achieve seven things:

1 Gain confidence

2 Jot down ideas for pieces you can write

3 Pick up some techniques and tips

4 Gain hard skills in travel journalism

5 Decide which will be the article you want to complete

6 Write that short travel piece

7 And send it off!

Your weekend toolkit

These are the things you need to get you started:

▶ A spiral bound notebook – a kind of personal log where you can begin, now, to write notes and ideas for travel pieces.

▶ Your laptop or PC, discs, a stack of white copy paper and spare ink cartridges.

▶ Guidebooks and magazines about " your" area – they could be *Lonely Planet* or *Rough Guides*, or local guidebooks and county magazines, local shopping guides and directories.

▶ Copies of the magazines and newspapers to which you'd like to sell your work – these could be local papers or the travel supplements published by national newspapers, or the travel or leisure sections of women's magazines.

▶ A good atlas.

▶ Plastic folders in which to keep cuttings, leaflets and notes.

▶ Large envelopes for sending work away – and stamps.

▶ Your own "business cards" with your name, details and the words *Travel Writer* on them – order them from www.vistaprint.co.uk.

▶ Music CDs from the country you're writing about – Greece, France, Spain, Italy? Or regional folk music or English classical music if you're writing about Britain.

▶ A new paperback novel – maybe one set in the place you're writing about – or fresh magazines to read and relax with at the end of the day.

Foreign flavours

If you've followed my *How to write for magazines… in one weekend* (Canal Street Publishing Ltd, £9.99, from www.canalstreet.org.uk) you'll know I recommend having delicious foods in your fridge for the weekend! You don't want to be popping out for supplies, clogging up your mind with finding a parking space and battling through crowds. You do want to have some tasty food in your fridge to look forward to – treats! Since you've already saved a good sum by not going away for your travel writing course, you can afford to spoil yourself just a little.

Get in the mood for your travel writing by stocking up with food and drink that conveys the flavours of the place you're writing about.

Writing about your holiday in France? You'll need croissants and apricot jam, chocolate croissants, French coffee (the scent will really inspire you), French cheese and French wine – you'll need a glass at the end of the day as you read through what you've done. How about a few – just a handful – of French chocolates from a chocolate cafe?

If Italy is your place, then some Italian pasta and sauce, cheeses and Frascati of course! Maybe you're writing about Greece? Lay in some tsatziki and Greek bread, salad, ready-made baklava, Greek yogurt and honey! You'll find Greek wine at Waitrose. Spain? There's a wonderful Spanish cheese called manchego. You could have Spanish olives and of course a little plate of tapas will go down well at the end of each day, maybe with a glass of good Spanish white. Morrison's do some great organic ones.

But what if you're writing about your local area? Then it's time to visit the local farmers' market or indoor market as if you were a tourist. Stock up with items that are exclusive to the area, indulge in them as if it's for the first time. Maybe the ingredients for a cream tea if you're in Devon or Cornwall, fresh fish if you live by the sea, all of the delicacies that you can buy in the North of England or the West Country. Just buying local eggs, honey and pastries will take you to the shops that could inspire some of your writing this weekend. In Bath, I buy locally-made chocolate fudge, Somerset cheeses and West Country sausage rolls!

Stock your fridge with items that need little cooking, a couple of bottles of mineral water, and some nibbles – fruits and nuts, to pick at while you're at your computer.

Your weekend timetable

Friday night – Make sure you have all you need for the weekend in your fridge. Do your food shopping Friday lunchtime, and use that time to buy any extra books or magazines that you need. Spend a little time on Friday evening relaxing and thinking in a positive way about this weekend – the weekend you will write a travel article!

Saturday – Aim for a productive but pleasurable day – maybe getting up after a short lie-in, ready to start at 10a.m. If you want to really get in the mood, you'll start with a shower using French bath products if you're writing about France, Greek ones if it's Greece (try www.korres.com for products) and so on. Then pick a breakfast that reflects the country you're in. Today, you'll be reading and making notes, but factor in a 30-minute walk round your block. No stopping for chats or buys – you're on your weekend course! As you work, you'll put the music of the country on your CD player.

Sunday – This is a day to review all you've read and written, and begin to polish your notes into something more solid. This is a day when you'll complete, check, print and even post your piece!

Write local

The easiest piece for you to write this weekend may well be about your own neighbourhood, whether it's a big city, a small town or a village. These pieces can sell well – to local and national magazines, magazines about tourism in the UK, and local newspapers. Or it could somewhere that you know very well, maybe a holiday spot you return to often, or somewhere you've recently visited and already have notes about. You'll need to be able to add the essential "factbox" of listings (more about these later) – but you can easily research these using websites.

If you're writing a local travel article, select something different and alternative. This doesn't mean the hippy trail! It means writing about your own town, city or neighbourhood while avoiding the conventional tourist destinations. For example:

- ▶ Docks areas – often redeveloped.

- ▶ Unusual churches and chapels – for example, Bristol has a Russian Orthodox church near its City Museum in the smart shopping district of Park Street, as well as an Eskimo church near Broadmead. Most cities have one or two quirky churches.

- ▶ Cheap or even free refreshments – Bath City Art Gallery has a coffee machine where you make your own drink for a few pence. There's a coffee shop on Pulteney Bridge where you can get a takeaway cappuccino for 80p and drink it overlooking one of England's most beautiful city river views.

- ▶ Well-hidden statues, shrines, gardens, parks and cafes which you, as a resident, know well, but which a visitor would be delighted to see.

- ▶ Gardens, terraces, waterfalls and lakes which are sometimes open to the public.

Picture this!

The best-written travel article in the world would be useless without pictures. The first question an editor asks after he or she has read a submitted piece and decides to accept it, is 'Where are the pictures?' If there aren't any, the feature won't be bought.

They can be prints, digital or slides – it's the clarity and content that counts, not the technical sophistication. You must also provide full information so that editors can write accurate captions for your photos. You need to say what the picture is of, and if it's a hotel or tourist attraction, give a contact number or website address so that readers could track it down. Offer as much help as you can to both the magazine staff handling your work, and to readers. And you should include some clear, smiling photographs of yourself. Make copies so you don't have to ask for them back. The photos you can get at Photo-Me booths are fine.

Top tip

Never be without a notebook and plenty of pens when you make a trip, even a local one. Write every day. Jot down small details – prices of coffee, music that's played, country etiquette and customs, as well as your own thoughts and impressions. Keep a folder of postcards, cards and leaflets.

Dream it!

How do you get the confidence and motivation you'll need? How do you get the vision of yourself as a travel writer?

This is a visualization given to me by Michael, my personal coach. I've used it many times over the years. What's wonderful about it is that there's no limit to the number of times you can do it. The more you use it, the more you will reinforce your will to write a travel article.

Sit quietly on your sofa, or stretch out on the floor. Your phone should be switched off. Breathe deeply and slowly. Picture a travel article with your name on, in a magazine or newspaper. Then see that publication in WH Smith's. Pick it up; feel it and even smell the scent of the glossy newsprint. Open it at your page. See your name. Make the vision big and bold. Smile as you look at your article.

It's important to try to get as many "senses" as you can into your visualisation – seeing, touching, smelling the distinctive scent of the glossy paper.

Return to this scene – and to your smile – any time you like.

Are you ready?

So – you've picked the place you want to write about!

You've equipped yourself with foods of the country.

Your new notebook is by your side.

You've done the visualization.

You've jotted down five ideas.

You've picked the one which most appeals.

You've thought about which magazine you will target.

You will send a picture of you.

And you will add a panel of listings… more on this later.

Yes, you will write a travel feature this weekend and send it off!

My first Golden Rule

Buy your first travel notebook now. Keep it with you at all times.

■ *Case study: How Julie did it*

At 22, **Julie Venis** is the youngest staff writer at Merricks Media (www.homesworldwide.co.uk) in Bath, which publishes a range of country magazines plus a raft of books. While still a creative writing student at Bath Spa University, I selected her to be the intern for my magazine, *Greece* – and she stayed with us for two years, working hard while she completed her degree. At the end of her time with me, she had disappointing news: there was no full-time job available for her.

Julie took temporary office jobs for six months, before competing for the next full-time job that came up – as editorial assistant on *Homes Worldwide*, one of the glossy magazines produced by Merricks Media.

I started writing at a very young age and had completed my first children's novel when I was 11 years old! I guess I was writing more out of therapy, though why I seemed to suffer from depression at such a young age, I have no idea!

My favourite subject at school had always been English, and I worked really hard to get into the top set. I was planning to finish my A-levels and then try to get a job at our local paper, but one of my friends urged me to go to university. Initially, I was looking at reading journalism, but during my A-level English Language and Literature courses, we had to do a creative writing module, and I decided to do that instead. I knew that some employers were sceptical about journalism or media courses, and I felt that combining English with creative writing would be more enjoyable and would put me in a better position in terms of job opportunities.

My choices were between Aberystwyth University and Bath Spa University College. I chose Aberystwyth, but after four months, I decided to transfer to Bath Spa, where I completed my degree – getting a 2:1 in Creative Studies in English with English Literature.

While at university, I was the intern for *Greece* magazine. I researched and wrote features and other items for the magazine. I also produced my own magazine, *Cyprus*, in my final year – which followed a similar format to *Greece*. I went to Cyprus to do the research and to take pictures. The magazine had travel features, property reports, an article about weddings, book reviews, food and drink, and much more.

I first discovered travel writing during the creative writing module of my A Levels. It was one of the options, and we had to read various travel pieces from some of the major newspapers (this was how we had to learn the craft). I then chose to write a travel feature in diary form about a vacation to South Africa (as this was one of the places that I most wanted to visit), and having never been there before, I had lots to research to do, but I think I managed it quite well and was pretty believable.

I'd hoped that my two years as intern for *Greece*, combined with the fact that I had (I felt!) successfully produced a whole travel magazine on Cyprus, would put me in good stead in the publishing world. I believed I would easily get a staff job at Merricks Media after university. But there was nothing. It was terribly disappointing – and a striking reminder that full-time jobs as travel writers are few and far between in today's publishing world.

I had to go around the temping agencies in Swindon, armed with my CV. It made me feel that those three years at uni were pointless, and the student debt I was carrying – almost £10,000 – made my situation even more depressing.

I did get temping work. I saved money, and sent off for prospectuses for fast-track magazine journalism courses. I felt that proper training might give me more of an edge over other candidates. I was also thinking about moving abroad. All sorts of ideas kept popping up!

At around this time – six months after I'd finished uni – I had an e-mail from Merricks Media's computer manager, with whom I'd kept in touch. He told me about a staff job at *Homes Worldwide* that was coming up. I went for an interview, after which I didn't hear anything for weeks. Then the editor left a voicemail message on my phone to ring her back. I did, and I'd got the job! In 2006, I went to Spain, Bulgaria and Dubai to write features for the magazine.

I write real life stories. Gathering in all of the property news is not so glamorous, but it's still great experience. Last year, I was asked to be a judge for *Greece* magazine's under-21 travel writing competition – a new feature that was my idea.

I always take my digital camera on trips; seeing my pictures on the page is as rewarding as seeing my writing in print. I take lots of pictures of just about everything – maybe too many. People shots are always very useful. You can normally get good landscape pictures from tourist offices, so I try to take pictures of the more unconventional if possible!'

These are my tips for new travel writers:

▶ Say what you see, not what you think readers will want to hear.

▶ Always pack a fresh new notebook for each trip.

▶ Let your personality shine through. You are only human after all, as are your readers.

▶ Sprinkle in some facts, but don't get bogged down in them. Use anecdotes and authentic conversations with the people you meet; they're often much more interesting than facts.

▶ Fix on a specific angle or theme for your piece before you start, and try to find an original slant if it's been used many times before.

▶ Don't use clichés – avoid them like the plague!

▶ Grab the reader's attention right from the very first sentence.

▶ Try to convey a sense of place, but without over-using adjectives.

My favourite writer is Sylvia Plath – you can see travel writing elements coming through in some of her work. It's fresh, original and vivid. ,

2 – Find ideas!

'It is not really possible to be out of ideas, since ideas can be found everywhere.'

~ Patricia Highsmith

You're settling into your weekend course. You've written notes about your writing plans, your ideas – and you. You've done the visualization. Now, perhaps, you need an idea for a trip, or an idea for tackling a feature about a trip you've already done. You have the facts and the impressions, yet you can't get started. Believe me, this isn't unusual.

In fact, there can be three problems, and you could have two of them: not having any ideas; having too many; or, having fixed on the topic, not knowing which angle to take. Ideas can rattle around in your mind. It's impossible to begin – even harder to finish. Which of your many visions is the right one? You sit down, get up, put music on, make a cup of coffee. You stare at your notes. You think about going out for a breath of fresh air – to clear your head. But this weekend you'll learn how to get an idea, corral it and anchor it.

Think strong

Getting ideas is all about energy and focus. Everyone wilts now and then. We all falter from time to time. These are my personal coaching tips for when your writing – and maybe your life – isn't going too well:

THINK strong, not weak. Don't think, 'It's hopeless, I'm too tired. It's too hard to think of anything to write'. Replace this with, 'I'm strong and I write well. I can do it'.

BE GLAD you've got this weekend just to write – and to be alive in!

IF you feel tense, rest on a sofa and let your body relax for a few minutes; listen to a short relaxation tape or soothing music. Then go back to the computer until it's time to stop!

TAKE a few minutes to tidy your workspace, so it will be fresh for you – you can do this at any time. I like the idea of having a few flowers on your desk, maybe a scented candle.

PLAY music that uplifts you – it could be anything from Eric Clapton to Vivaldi.

DON'T aim to be perfect, just productive. Above all… write.

Dodging the demons

Depression, fatigue and disappointment can clobber your resolve. Many writers suffer from occasional bouts of mild depression which play havoc with their work. If you have a demanding, full-time job, it may be that you can just about manage during the week, but stagger into the weekend feeling tired, flat and drained of energy. You can't even think about writing.

It may be that disappointment and rejection have got you down. It could be to do with your writing, or with something else – but whatever it is may drain your vitality and energy for writing.

There are things you can do to help yourself. To tackle these demons, we need to let go of the 'stand and deliver' attitude to life – the attitude that insists 'I must never be annoyed by anyone… insulted… rejected… treated badly'. The list goes on; my own 'must never' list on a bad day can be as long as a telephone directory!

That 'stand and deliver' challenge to life was often instilled by parents who were overly protective in ensuring that their children were never subjected to insults, rejection and bad treatment. They wanted only the best for their children, but in later years this can work against you as a writer. Rejection is an unavoidable part of the writing package – you have to be able to handle it. If you're too crushed or angered by it, if 'stand and deliver' is too ingrained in you, you'll never submit or even finish magazine features; you'll be expecting magazine editors to be ringing you with choice commissions! If you spend too much time seething over imagined or real insults, you'll never start writing! You'll never feel like it; you'll be too fed up and angry.

You can replace the 'musts' with more rational thinking. 'I must not be rejected ever' could be replaced with, 'I would much prefer not to be rejected, but if I am, I can take it, because there are no guarantees in life!'

Use self -reaffirmation more often and consciously:

'I tried my best with my article; being rejected does not mean I am no good.'

'My style did not match their requirements or preferences this time. Yes, I'd prefer not to have the piece rejected, but I can take it!'

Sleeping lion

Lack of sleep – with troubled minds kept awake by tumbling thoughts and worries – can be another obstacle to writing. But you need to balance the hours staring at the computer with some activity.

So, add a little exercise to your hours in front of that computer! Even a brisk half-hour walk around the block will help you sleep later on. Then in the evening, try a relaxation tape – *You Are Amazing* is a free CD of hypnotic suggestions included in the paperback *You Can Be Amazing* by Ursula James (Century, £9.99)

I recommend a glass of warm milk, with my Brighton friend Dr Milind Jani's almonds and nutmeg mix (Peaceful sleep mixture – www.pavilionhealth. co.uk), or try a fortifier such as his Energy Plus… you take a spoonful or two daily for energy and prevention of infections.

If you've been feeling seriously down – too down to write anything, but hoping this weekend will kick-start your energy – I can recommend a homeopathic remedy, New Era tissue salts. They're billed "for nervous exhaustion and general debility" and cost £4.49 for 450 tablets. You can take three doses of four tiny tablets each, or more if you like – you can't overdose on them, and they don't cause side effects.

If you've had a lot of stress, then they're well worth a try – they've worked for me, brilliantly. It's a great chemical-free way to lift yourself from stress-related weariness. And you'll find them in good health food shops.

When you're lying awake with a churning mind, it's better to get up and make notes in your personal coaching diary. List the problems and write down some 'automatic' thoughts about them. Write through the problem.

Don't forget, though, that you don't have to be completely comfortable to start writing. It helps if you are – yet you can begin even if things aren't absolutely perfect. You'll find that as you read and jot notes down, warmth begins to creep over you – you're making progress. And before too long, the act of working, and writing, creates its own energy. The work of writing is a mood-lifter! It's probably the cheapest one there is – with no side effects. It can even help to write down your problems in a letter to yourself. But visualise only the positive! *"I see myself getting up at 7.30, finishing 2 pages of notes on my travel article. I am productive and content."* Write down these positive thoughts.

Mood-lifters for free!

Four things to make you feel more optimistic in the next five minutes . . .

1 Know that you can make a 'soft entry' with a travel feature – it doesn't have to be placed in a travel magazine. You can aim for a local magazine or newspaper, a woman's magazine, the travel and leisure section of a national newspaper.

2 Remember that travel features with a personal angle – for example a holiday as a single, a first holiday with a baby, a learning-a-language holiday – could be placed in a number of different journals, and sold more than once. Any feature in which you can give readers practical tips from your own experience stands a good chance of being accepted.

3 Activity holidays are a big draw – they could be anything from learning to scuba dive in the Caribbean to pony trekking in Wales.

4 Focus on this – travel magazine editors always welcome the new face, the new voice. There's always, always a shortage of "the perfect freelance". You could be the one they've been waiting for.

Spark ideas

Feeling better? Begin to think now about the type of holiday you'd like to have – as well as the place that you'll write about. You don't have to write a thing, just make notes!

Settle down with current newspapers and magazines. Look at review pages for new books and new films. Are any set somewhere you could research and write about? Study the business pages of your local papers. Are regional airports offering new routes cheaply? For example, the introduction of new easyJet routes from Bristol made me realise that it would be possible for me to travel for the weekend to Naples, Seville or Berlin – all for about £40. Any one of these would make a great '48 hours in'… feature for local and national papers.

Think of a complete getaway in Britain. Is there somewhere near you where readers can get away from it all – with no phone and no noise? It could be a remote moor, an island, a monastery retreat. Don't forget – think about the type of holiday you could do, as well as the place where it'll be.

Here are five great ideas to get you thinking:

1   Activity breaks will always be a good bet – cookery, painting, walking or fitness holidays, perhaps written as a diary, from a first person point of view. Point out any downsides as well as all the pluses. For example, the second day of my yoga holiday in Greece was my low point – I felt hot and tired and no one spoke to me. On the second evening I joined in some Greek dancing and got to know a couple of people who were also on their own, and suddenly the holiday was a good idea after all! When you're on a course on your own, always join in any dancing. It really frees you, and you'll find friends – make the effort.

2   Never forget the pulling power of the list. Here's how you could do it – just writing a list. Can you come up with four perfect beaches in the north of England, six retreats in the UK, and eight great cafes in a city? You may not need more than a listing (that's an address, phone number, perhaps a website address, and prices) and a couple of descriptive and accurate lines about them.

3   Travel in a different way. Did you do a trip by rail or sea or car that's normally done by air? This would make a good read. Many holidaymakers dislike flying and would be interested to see how feasible and pleasant a rail or sea journey can be.

4   Can you do a holiday on the cheap, with prices pruned to the bone or, if you are being treated, in Gold Card style? Why not write about your romantic weekend in Berlin? (Romance? Berlin? Why not? Always go for the opposite to the cliché weekend in Paris or Venice!). Is there a feature in your £15-a-day rail trip through Greece? Of course there is.

5   Food and wine are important – in fact, if you can write about your cookery holiday in Tuscany, your gastro course in Vietnam or your wine workshops in Florence, you could hit the jackpot. You can never write too much about food and wine.

Top tip

An activity holiday, let's say a cooking course, can be re-cycled – once as a travel piece, once in a mainstream women's magazine, again in a food magazine. Keep broadening the scope of your outlets.

Going solo?

Must you be with someone to travel? No – not necessarily. Many thousands of people now travel on their own. Lots of us actually prefer it! You may have heard of that old Chinese saying: 'The man who goes alone can start the day, but he who travels with another must wait till the other is ready.' There's no doubt that you'll get more out of a trip – much more to write about – if you are on your own. You'll notice more, speak to more people, make new friends, and do more things. As part of a couple, you naturally focus on your partner for much of the time.

Travelling independently, you have no option but to focus on your destination. Travel alone is empowering. It's exhilarating. It's freedom. But it can also be a bit daunting, especially if you haven't done too much of it.

Even when you choose to take a holiday by yourself, you still need more confidence than when you travel as part of a couple. If you're a novice solo traveller, start by just planning some days out on your own – maybe a rail trip to a big city, or a coach journey into the country. Take a long, scenic, bus trip, have lunch out, then take the bus back. Try a train trip to a beauty spot or to a city you haven't spent time in before. Take notes as you go – the day out, with lots of tips and listings, is a good prospect for a travel piece.

My tip for a solo travel-writing holiday is to look at short city breaks where you'll have lots to do and see, and you will be energised by the city buzz.

The two-day trip – A weekend trip to Paris by Eurostar is easy to do. You avoid the stress of flying, and with the right deal you may be able to upgrade to first class comfort for one leg of the journey. In Paris, the Marais and Left Bank districts are more relaxing and interesting than the city centre. Paris is full of churches to explore… that could be a topic. Or bookshops, art galleries or street markets. Go for the ones that don't feature much in the published guides – create your own, new listings. Other good weekend venues for solo travellers? Try Bristol, Cheltenham, Bath, York, Edinburgh or Oxford – all comfortable places of great beauty and designed for walking. London is perfect if you have the right hotel – pick one from Ladies In London, from £49 B & B. (Call 0870 770 8181 or visit www.thehoteldirectory.co.uk).

A week alone – New York is a city that's very comfortable for men and women on their own – there are so many of them! Hotel rooms are surprisingly quiet and well insulated, with excellent room service. Central Park has cafes, restaurants, walks and gardens, tearooms – then there's cinema, theatre and music. You need never go near a department store unless you want to. It has more bookstores – both new and second hand – than any other western city. The Museum of Modern Art is a must, and you could try the South Street seaport district for a terrace lunch and riverside views.

It's a city made for walking, with an easy grid system, lovely for a late summer or autumn break… and there's a story for travel writers on almost every street!

Homework – plan ahead

PLAN your timetable carefully and treat yourself to extras, such as books and meals out, at your holiday venue. Pack at least two fresh notebooks, plenty of pens and a camera. Record your experiences all the time, and jot down useful contact details for readers who might want to holiday alone.

WRITE ahead to the local tourist offices: get all the information and maps you can.

COURSES which last all day may be too tiring – opt for a half-day course, leaving you with a half-day free.

ENSURE you have as much hotel comfort as you need – for example, a balcony, roof garden, hair dryer. As a writer, you need a peaceful and relaxing hotel room. It's worth paying extra for a balcony or roof garden.

CREATE your own holiday around a festival or celebration, such as the Edinburgh Fringe or the Cheltenham Literature Festival. The event hosts can usually suggest accommodation options.

Confidence boosting tips for the solo travel writer…

▶ Order a room service breakfast if going downstairs alone seems daunting – or just have morning coffee out. Book a hotel room with a balcony so you can sit out with coffee.

▶ Chat to various people on a course – don't get tied up with one person too soon. Most relaxing courses are cookery, art and crafts.

▶ Eating alone worries you? If the weather is good or you are abroad, lunch out at a pavement bistro is much more relaxing. Treat yourself to a glass of wine – and have your notebook with you.

▶ Book tickets to a concert, theatre or cinema – you actually won't feel lonely. Plus, you can choose just what you want to see – no compromises… and write about it.

Four top tips for magazine ideas . . .

1   Don't use too topical an idea for a specialist magazine. These magazines may come out only four times a year or every other month. They stay around longer, but features based on most news events may look out-of-date very quickly. Pick more general, but still modern, themes or trends.

2   Think *benefits*. Professional magazines look at features – and cover lines – in terms of the benefits they offer the reader. So don't just think of a travel idea, develop it into something that will benefit the reader, such as learning a language on a holiday course, a budget holiday that saves them money, timesaving packing tips, or ways of turning a holiday into a job.

3   Anything that can be picked out as a coverline – used on the magazine's cover – will be even more tempting to the editor you're trying to impress. Use *number* pieces – 5 retreat holidays; 7 ways to solo travel success: 6 perfect destinations less than an hour from home.

4   Include tips, unusual facts, hints, panels of concise information, do's and don'ts. They make the page look good and readers love them.

My second Golden Rule

Decide what you'll do for your travel article and where you'll go. Jot down three angles on it now.

■ *Case study: How Paul did it*

Paul Jenner, travel author and journalist

There weren't many jobs for aspiring novelists or playwrights, so at 18 I settled for the next best thing and began training as a journalist on my local newspaper, *The Southend Standard*. It soon became clear that I wasn't very good at keeping my foot in someone else's front door, and after a couple of years I left. It was about ten years before I returned to writing, and I've been doing it ever since. I wouldn't recommend it to anyone as a way of earning a living but, as a freelance, you can enjoy an enviable lifestyle.

I live in the foothills of the Spanish Pyrenees with my partner Christine Smith, who is also a writer. If it's a beautiful day (and, unfortunately, it often is a beautiful day where we live) we might decide to go riding or skiing or swimming. Of course, we have to make up for it by working till late at night and all weekend, but that's fine with us. That's what I mean by an enviable lifestyle.

We've written several books together. Previously, we lived in France for about seven years and both speak French fairly easily, but with lots of mistakes. We've also now acquired some Spanish.

The skill I'm most proud of is the ability, in an emergency, to trim a horse's hoof and nail a shoe on, basically because it's just not the kind of thing I ever would have imagined myself doing 20 years ago. I'm also pretty pleased that I've learned to ride a horse, sail a boat, dive, ski and snowboard. I think it's very important to try lots of different things, and lots of different places, because you can't know what you really want until you've experienced everything.

I'd always wanted to travel and try different things, but it was very difficult to afford interesting holidays; most writers don't earn very much. At the time, I was a jobbing freelance writer, turning out features for magazines and press releases for public relations companies. I saw that the only way I was going to get to travel was if somebody else paid. But I also very quickly learned that magazines and newspapers were awash with travel articles sent in by just about anybody who had ever held a bucket and spade. So my first travel piece was for a magazine called *Conferences & Exhibitions International*, a rather specialist market which precluded amateurs. There I had the good fortune to meet up with a woman who taught me exactly how the whole business worked at that time – essentially, how to get free flights and hotel rooms.

When Chrissie and I got together about 20 years ago, we had the idea that it would be better to live in a country for a while rather than just visit for a few days. Until then, we'd both been doing the press trips thing, which involved spending two or three days somewhere and then proclaiming yourself an expert. So we began in the French Alps. Then we moved to the French Pyrenees. Then to the Spanish Pyrenees. That's where the plan went wrong. The next stop was supposed to be Morocco but, instead, we gradually acquired an old stone-built water mill, five ponies, three sheep and two dogs and got ourselves stuck. Meanwhile, we wrote all about the Pyrenees: the very first edition of *The Rough Guide to the Pyrenees; Berlitz Discover Pyrenees* and *Landscapes of the Pyrenees*. Since then we've also written *Landscapes of the Ebor Delta; The Landscapes Walking Companion; Au Revoir Angle Terre*, which is about living abroad; and *Ditch the Donkey*, a guidebook to unusual holiday ideas. A follow-up called *Bin the Bucket and Spade* was published by White Ladder Press, and *The Outdoor Bible* will follow.

When you're living abroad, getting work is very difficult. Ideally you need to be on the scene in London. You can spend as much time trying to get work as actually doing the work. That's why I nowadays mostly write books. One book can keep you busy for a few months, but one article keeps you busy for only a day or so.

I've always seen travel (as opposed to a holiday) as a way of experiencing new places, activities and ideas. So as I travel around, I always try to find out what people in different cultures do and think. For example, do Hindus in India all follow the Karma Sutra? Do people in California all practice the Tao of sex? Are people in Malaysia happier than people in Manchester? To me, that's travel writing just as much as hotels and monuments. Then I can incorporate my findings into my writing. For example, I recently wrote *Teach Yourself Great Sex*, published by Hodder. And I'm currently working on *Teach Yourself Happiness*.

When I was working as a freelance travel journalist for newspapers and magazines, I was away every week. It could get completely mad. I remember returning from a week's trip to the Canadian Rockies and leaving the next day for the Gulf. It's a great life for a single person for a while, but that kind of lifestyle is ruinous for relationships. Nor do you really get to learn very much about the countries you're visiting. Nowadays, Chrissie and I always travel together and we would never go anywhere for less than a week. The ideal is a month or more.

When I was a staff journalist, I had to learn to write fast but, of course, there was always a sub-editor to tidy things up. As a freelance, you can't submit features that are much less than perfect, so you write more slowly. My record as a freelance was 6,000 published words written in less than 24 hours. I didn't go to bed and I remember leaving the house around four o'clock in the morning to catch a flight to Madrid. Crazy! Now I'm a slow writer. I work like a sculptor, getting down the broad shape first and then adding and subtracting. I find it hard to produce more than 1,000 polished words a day.

Ideally, you need to be friends with your editors. You need to be meeting them in the pub. It's not essential, but it certainly helps. As always, it's not just what you know, but who you know. Apart from that, you obviously have to supply accurate articles written in the right style for the publication and delivered on time. If you're lucky enough to get someone to commission you, it's important to remember that that person's neck may be on the chopping block if you mess up. So don't mess up.

Ernest Hemingway is the master. He writes one sentence and you see, hear, smell, taste and touch everything. Apart from that, Hemingway was one of the few writers who actually enjoyed being alive. So many write about how everything went wrong and how miserable they are. Personally, I'm not interested in writers who find life a burden.

The big problem of travel writing is the cost of travel. It's extremely difficult to earn a living as a freelance travel writer. You might, for example, make a trip lasting a week and sell one article for, say, £200. The freelance solution is to get several articles out of one trip; and not all of them necessarily travel articles.

Paul Jenner, El Moli, Espolla, Girona, Spain, E-17753. Tel: 00 34 972 193 183, e-mail HYPERLINK mailto:pauljenner@terra.es pauljenner@terra.es

3 – Any journey is travel!

'I haven't been everywhere, but it's on my list.'

~ Susan Sontag

One of your worries this weekend might have been that travel writing is really about foreign places – the more exotic the better – and that because you don't often go abroad, or even very far from home in Britain, you can't really "do" travel. Think again. I want to convince you that every single time you leave your home, you're embarking on a journey – and one you could write about. Walking across your town or city, going to the seaside for a day, or to a nearby shopping centre – you're travelling! Taking a train to work, a coach for a day out, by car to a supermarket… each and every journey is travel. Anything and everything could throw up an adventure. You'll be in a different mood for each journey, you could see things with more clarity. Sometimes there can be an intensity to the simplest journey – a focus that will aid your writing. Remember, the streets and sights which are familiar to you will be new and different to your reader. Keep that notebook with you at all times.

Take a look at this extract from a famous novel, if you don't believe me!

> *Away, with a shriek and a roar and a rattle, from the town, burrowing among the dwellings of men and making the streets hum, flashing out into the meadows for a moment, mining in through the damp earth, booming on in darkness and heavy air, bursting out again into the sunny day so bright and wide: away, with a shriek, and a roar, and a rattle, through the fields, through the woods, through the corn, through the hay, through the chalk, through the mould, through the clay, through the rock, among objects close at hand and almost in the grasp, ever*

flying from the traveller, and a deceitful distance ever moving slowly with him: like as in the track of the remorseless monster, Death!

Through the hollow, on the heights, by the heath, by the orchard, by the park, by the garden, over the canal, across the river, where the sheep are feeding, where the mill is going, where the barge is floating, where the dead are lying, where the factory is smoking, where the stream is running.

Breasting the wind and light, the shower and sunshine, away, and still away, it rolls and roars, fierce and rapid, smooth and certain: and great works and massive bridges crossing up above, fall like a beam of shadow an inch broad upon the eye and then are lost.

Away with a shriek and a roar and a rattle plunging down into the earth again, and working on in such a storm of energy and perseverance, that amidst the darkness and whirlwind the motion seems revered, and to tend furiously backward until a ray of light upon the wet wall shows its surface flying past like a fierce stream.

Away once more into the day and through the day with a shrill yell of exultation, roaring rattling tearing on, spurning everything with its dark breath, sometimes pausing for a minute where a crowd of faces are, that in a minute more are not: sometimes lapping water greedily, and before the spout at which it drinks has ceased to drip upon the ground, shrieking roaring rattling though the purple distance!

Louder and louder yet, it shrieks and cries as it comes tearing on resistless to the goal: and now its way, still like the way of Death, is strewn with ashes thickly. Everything around is blackened. There are dark pools of water, muddy lanes and miserable habitations far below. There are jagged walls and falling houses close at hand, and through the battered roofs and broken windows, wretched rooms are seen, where want and fever hide themselves in many wretched shapes, while smoke, and crowded gables, and distorted chimneys, and deformity of brick and mortar penning up deformity of mind and body, choke the murky distance. As Mr Dombey looks out of his carriage window, it is never in his thoughts that the monster who has brought him here has let the light of day in on these things: not made or caused them. It was the journey's fitting end, and might have been the end of everything, it was so ruinous and dreary.

That was Charles Dickens, writing in the 1840s, when in the character of Mr Dombey, he was getting his first experience of the steam railway age, on a train from London to Leamington Spa. To travellers then, taking a train was as traumatic and as fascinating as our first plane journeys in the next century. They found the experience strange, almost magical – yet terrifying. Before trains, they were used only to the slow clip clop of a horse and the rumbling wheels of a carriage or cart. The extreme noise and speed of a train, the way it covered so much ground so quickly, was sensational.

Dickens' take on a mid-19th century train journey is as fresh and as vibrant now as the day he wrote it. Of course, his prose is more expansive than we are accustomed to, yet I am sure a modern equivalent would work too. He records both the rail journey, what he sees from the carriage as it speeds across the English counties, and his inner journey. Someone he loved had died; he was depressed and miserable. As always, your inner feelings are still with you wherever you travel; even the brilliant sunshine, charm and natural beauty of Capri or Crete will seem bitter sweet if you are in a sad mood. But for a writer, that's fine – you share your feelings, knowing that all of us have felt the same – at some time, somewhere. Don't deny those feelings – get them down on paper.

Roads much travelled

Travel that seems at first to be commonplace need not be; it can be a route to original writing with which readers can identify. Everyone makes these ordinary journeys, but we don't all see them in exactly the same way. And it's these features about the glamorous places that haven't been written to death, and the journeys that are lesser known, which you are more likely to sell. Look at the old docks areas, the hidden curiosities in city districts that aren't fashionable yet have fascinating stories to tell. What is there about these forgotten places and the ordinary journeys we make around and through them that may excite the interest of travel editors bored with romantic weekends in Paris and Prague, weddings in Santorini and Venice and shopping holidays in New York and Vienna?

How do you make seemingly ordinary journeys into something that's certain to make an editor's eyes light up? In Britain, it's hard to find journeys that are more mundane than the ones you'll have on motorways, whether they're long haul trips from London to Glasgow or daily commuter rides along stretches of the M25. To demonstrate that any journey can provide you with a piece of travel writing, here are some examples from *The Guardian*, which asked a team of writers to describe their journeys on different parts of the country's motorway network. Mundane? Functional? No, their writing sparkles! Notice how every writer includes all the senses – sight, touch, smell and hearing. It's such an unusual and winning take on travel.

M2 – the panoramic one (Zoe Williams)

Let me talk you through the beauty of it: as you join it from the south, it has five mighty lanes. There is never any traffic. The only bad thing that can happen to you is that you run out of petrol on the one farthest from the hard shoulder. That happened to me once, and when the AA man arrived he assumed my sister (27) and my brother (23) were my children. This is one of the top five bad days of my life. It is testament to the motorway's healing powers that it has remained my favourite motorway.

… Services-wise, there ain't much meat on her, but what is there is choice, as Spencer Tracey used to say of Katharine Hepburn, in his not-at-all demeaning account of their life-long love affair. Medway is a Moto. Its loos are very clean, on account of the rigorous, no-nonsense natures of the people of Thanet. To my knowledge, it has never run out of the key sections of pick 'n mix, unlike some services I could mention, which run out of white mice almost immediately, but don't actually bother replacing any until they're down to their last chocolate brazil. It was among the first motorway stations to start proselytizing about fruit portions over the distracting olfactory hum of frying bacon.

M4 – the boring one (Tim Dowling)

Hurtling along the westbound carriage while listening to a You and Yours segment about landmarks, I realise that this is precisely what the M4 lacks: a series of easily recognisable features that tell you how far you have come, and how far you have to go. Yes, there is the occasional restored tithe barn which, on closer inspection, turns out to be the cupola of a gigantic Tesco. There is the hulking secure-storage facility on the horizon which, if the exit signs are to be believed, is Windsor Castle. There is the smell from the sewage-treatment plant, which is for many motorway users their only abiding memory of Slough … for the most part, the M4 is an uninterrupted ribbon of quasi-bucolic tedium demarcated only by its numbered junctions and soulless corporate headquarters.

… Facilities include an M&S Simply Food, a new and groovily-appointed restaurant called Fork in the Road, a Caffe Ritazza, a Burger King, a WH Smith, an Upper Crust and a barbershop. The worst or at least the most pointless is Heston Services – depressingly down at heel and too close to London. If you are heading for the city, you can probably wait until you get there. If you are leaving London, it is too soon to stop. Just carry on west – Chieveley or bust!

M5 – the holiday highway (Patrick Barkham)

Life, the band St Etienne reckoned, was like a motorway, "dull, grey and long – till he came along". But the 162.9 miles of the M5 are sprinkled with stardust. Flowing, as the signs say, to "the SOUTH WEST", the M5 not only featured in Fawlty Towers, where an American guest called it "a little back street", but its Taunton Deane service area is said to be patronised by Lenny Henry and Dawn French.

… The motorway is the Jade Goody of the network – a good-time-loving loudmouth who tramples on national treasures … those who bemoan the uniformity of motorway services have obviously never set tyre on the M5. There is the mini-Stansted airport of Strensham (southbound), the well-forested cosiness of Michaelwood, the stripped-pine sauna effect of Sedgemoor and the garden-centre-style-chic of Exeter services.

M6 – the non-nonsense one (John Harris)

My first stop is at Charnock Richard, a services that sounds as if it was named after an obscure folk singer. Near the Coffee Primo outlet, a young man in a baseball cap is looking askance at a breakfast of leek and potato soup. This is Jocque, a 21-year-old South African, en route from Kent to Perthshire. He has spent the night in the car park. "I got a proper five hours' sleep: you put in earplugs, and it's fine." This won't be the last time today that peering below the surface reveals an itinerant subculture, seeing out too much of their lives in forecourts and car parks.

M11 – the mysterious one (Stuart Jeffries)

The M11 is like life. It starts mysteriously and ends at a crematorium. The M11 is a mystery because it doesn't start at junction 1 like sensible motorways, but at junction 4. Why?

… we plump for the Coffee Primo concession where my blueberry muffin looks like underlay and tastes of nothing. The cappuccino is hot and tastes of nothing … best place to eat … your car.

M23 – the short one (Leo Hickman, who chose to hitchhike – and that's another way of doing a journey!)

I used to thumb rides along this very route as a student, and a foolish curiosity to investigate the art of hitching has led me to see whether I've still got the knack. Now I remember why I ended up choosing the trains. Pease Pottage is the only service station along the M23 … given the billing, I'm disappointed to see that the chewable toothbrush dispenser has been ripped from the

> *wall. After buying a tin of sour lemons at WH Smith – a place*
> *so well-stocked with women's erotic literature that the section*
> *requires a whole shelf to itself – I head back out to the Shell petrol*
> *station and hold out a piece of cardboard with "lon'n" etched in*
> *out in marker pen. Someone, anyone, please take me home.*

These travel pieces about Britain's boring, mundane and much-used motorways are amusing, intriguing and informative. These writers notice every little detail, which is the mark of an excellent travel writer. You can too – now you know how!

Starting off…

Whether you're writing about holidays in faraway places or journeys nearer home, give the start of your feature a 'short story' quality! Capture the reader's attention with an introduction that could just as easily be the opening passage of a piece of fiction.

Zoom in on one incident, one situation, one event and give it more detail, more colour, more feeling. Take one aspect and open it up, as you would with a short story. Be honest. Travel, as well as being wonderful, often frays tempers! Don't gloss over setbacks and irritations.

Here's how you do it. Write your piece in the first person. Give your introduction a 'must read on' quality, a promise of something intriguing to come. Here are three examples:

1   It was when the ticket inspector told me my train was actually going to Edinburgh, not St. Albans as I'd thought, that I realised rail travel can offer some unexpected opportunities.

2   "Champagne? Welcome!" The smiling naval officer ushered us up the gangplank. All we'd been doing was standing at sunset staring at a Greek frigate armed with Cruise missiles docked in Halki harbour. But suddenly we were guests at a party. It pays to dress up a bit for dinner – even on a Greek island.

3   I didn't expect to spend part of my holiday on Paxos helping the island doctor to stitch up my partner's foot! Only a man would wander into a ruined house and fiddle about with a boarded-up window until the massive piece of rotting wood fell on him. But – those two years as a Red Cross cadet in a baggy navy and white uniform really paid off! I couldn't have been more flattered when the Greek doctor applauded my non-squeamish approach. The thing is, he was very good looking. So the poor patient was somewhat ignored as we made flirtatious conversation across the operating table.

With the 'must read on' quality, the 'short story intro', the rest of the feature becomes simple. You don't have to actually create a short story – it's just the introduction to your article, to tempt the reader in and set the theme and tone. But of course, when you have the idea, there's no reason why you shouldn't later on write a short story based, too, on that journey.

Always think of travel writing as offering you future writing possibilities – a general feature, an opinion piece, a short story. Travel is life itself – so there are so many possibilities! Keep breathing, keep moving, keep writing...

Words and pictures

▶   A small rucksack is the best way to carry things – pack a small notebook, pens, camera and a plastic envelope folder for all the leaflets, cards, brochures you'll collect

▶   Ask café owners and restaurant staff for recipes you've enjoyed

▶   Visit the local tourist office, chat to the staff and pick up any material they offer

▶   Write in your notebook every day: you need not begin to write the article, but record what you did and where you went – you could forget. Make sure you note down details – prices of shrimp sandwiches in St Ives, the cost of a metro pass in Paris, how much a basic museum lunch would set you back in London – everything readers might like to know.

▶   Take pictures – not just landscapes, but of small details such as that brass doorknocker in the shape of an angel, the cocktail intricately decorated with fruit and flowers, the painted tiles around a fountain.

Journeys direct

19 ideas for "any journey" travel writing you could do next weekend!

1   Research your local churches and chapels. Does your town or city have any very old or unusual synagogues? Look at their booklets, see what they offer visitors – cafes, bookshops, book sales? You need only four or five to make a feature. See if you can add a couple of "people" pictures, maybe of local vicars or choristers.

2   Sampled a training restaurant? Every big city has one. It's where trainee chefs and waiters learn their trade, with real diners, in a mocked-up restaurant within a city college. Fun to do, fun to write about – and you're giving readers good value, because the prices are much lower than normal restaurants, and the food is often just as good!

3   Book the cheapest airline ticket from your local airport – could be to Krakow, Dusseldorf, Antwerp, Linz – somewhere not immediately obvious as a holiday destination.

4   Try returning to the place where you were born, or where you grew up. What's changed – and what's interesting about it?

5   Can you visit all of the museums in your city in one weekend, maybe during the period in which they have free entry?

6   Take a day out at a local spa – just spend a day there.

7   Got a free bus pass? Lucky you – yes really! That bus pass could take you, for instance, all over Wales or all round the West Country. Just see where it takes you and what you can write about.

8   Anniversary coming up? Want to do something unconventional? I spent a recent Christmas Day in Venice, thanks to a cheap flight from my local airport – lunching on spaghetti bolognese and a glass of prosecco, sitting by the Grand Canal. In the evening, we went to a Vivaldi concert in a church. We had a wonderful time the whole week – no shopping, no trees, and no turkey.

9   Secret gardens in your city – there will be some. See what you can find.

10 Does your city have film, music or literary festivals? Go to a few events and write about them.

11 Are you planning a Big Trip to visit friends or relatives you haven't seen for ages? That could be a gripping travel feature.

12 Farmers' markets and organic markets – are there some locally? Pick out the five best stalls.

13   Learn to swim or ride a horse later in life – you'll find a class locally. Try a Saturday or Sunday!

14   Leave the car in the garage and just walk, walk, walk for a weekend.

15   Volunteer for something in your town for one day – maybe collecting for charity, cooking at a hostel, helping out at a hospital

16   Invest in one perfect cappuccino, sitting outside an expensive bar! Here's where you'll make your notes for the weekend.

17   Like vintage clothes? The big cities have some good second-hand clothes shops, and some of the best are in World's End stretch of London's King's Road.

18   Look ahead to an upcoming anniversary of a poet, writer or composer whose name is strongly associated with a locality, such as DH Lawrence and Nottingham, Dylan Thomas and South Wales, and less well known ones – such as an Enid Blyton or Agatha Christie anniversary.

19   Sample a monastery or a silent retreat. I recommend these as being uplifting for your soul, as well as giving you space and freedom to write – and to learn about the lives of those who've made their home there. Visit www.retreats.org.uk to find a retreat that's right for you

Getting it written!

You've got notes for a local journey, a local travel project, but you're having trouble concentrating and finishing it. How I sympathise! I've experienced this: starting, stopping, doing little chores, going out for a newspaper, anything that distracts you from the vital task of finishing your travel article.

Here's a tip – try complete silence, instead of background music or the radio, for a change. The energising qualities of silence – and the way it aids concentration – are a vital part of my life, both when working and relaxing. Complete quiet also offers something healing and mystical: it's sad that young people are becoming uncomfortable with it.

There are ways of finding, or creating, quiet places for yourself in our noisy world. These are a few ideas of mine.

Learn to wake up, and get up, early. Spiritual masters of every discipline know the value of this – not only can you get more done, but the world has a peace and quality at dawn that's lost during the rest of the day. You could get a number of chores done in wonderful peace and quiet, well before the family wake – or simply use this quiet time for a walk or reading.

Quaker meeting houses, yoga centres and museums often have quiet cafes and peaceful tiny gardens. Seek out your local quiet "alternative" for a lunchtime coffee instead of fighting it out at the sandwich shop. You can think about your writing then – the writing you'll do in the evening or at the weekend. You can write down your goals for the week ahead – and stick to them!

Cut down your television viewing hours, and free up more time for your writing. Most telly soaps and dramas feature argumentative, noisy people and loud music, and watching them can be a time-wasting habit. A long bus ride can be more relaxing than train or car. Find out what local bus companies have to offer – a cheap half-day or day trip to somewhere different and peaceful? It's something you might be able to do while your children are at school, or you have a free day… and write about it.

Write a diary every day – choose a tranquil time and get your thoughts on paper. Morning writing will refresh you. Every weekend make a list of "quiet things" you plan to do during the following week. The more peace you can get into your life, the more rewarding it will be… and the more writing you'll get done. *Write it Down, Make it Happen* (Henriette Anne Klauser, Simon & Schuster, $10, 2001) offers practical and spiritually uplifting advice for achieving your goals.

My third Golden Rule:

Do a free local travel journey next week – with your notebook in hand.

■ *Case study: How Bob did it*

Bob Jenkins, magazine and newspaper travel writer.

Leaving school in 1965, I started out as a scientist but later blundered into an array of jobs including accounts clerk, youth hostel warden, advice centre manager and publishing assistant for a small, excruciatingly dull technical magazine. I also travelled a lot and wrote hopeless novels that were never published.

My first piece in print was a deliberately bizarre short travel story in my employer's ultra-staid in-house newsletter. The second, on follies in Bath, where I live, was published in a regional glossy magazine. Seeing them in print was a thrill and gave me encouragement. The moral is, get something published, even if it's in the church or village newsletter – it's a start.

Some local daily newspapers run features by contributors in weekend travel pages, especially if the material is free. Weekly papers may be interested in articles on attractions, gardens and museums close to home. There's nothing to stop you writing a travel article about your own stamping ground.

One small step can be a giant leap. Just a single piece submitted to *The Bath Chronicle* in 1987 led to thousands over the following 20 years on topics ranging from sport, humour and comment to days out, travel and local history. It also led to travel pieces in national newspapers and magazines. My first piece in a national paper came about because it fell on the editor's desk the very day he was looking for material on that area – Devon. Lucky, yes, but only in part. My piece on green tourism was carefully targeted and in a suitable style, length and format. I also made sure I sent it to the right person.

It's a waste of time to casually e-mail the same piece to different outlets without studying the publication or finding out how the travel editor operates. This is a very competitive business; you must do the groundwork.

Personal contacts are crucial. You have to exploit any opening. Put fresh ideas to anyone you have met or people who have published your work before. In today's hard-pressed publishing world, promptness, reliability and accuracy count for a lot. Editors don't have time to rewrite, reorganize, check facts and hunt for photographs. You must make their life easy – or as easy as possible.

Over the past two decades, I have written about places from Tunbridge Wells to Tallinn, Chester to the Caribbean and holiday from luxury cruising to youth hostelling. Latterly, my focus has been more on the UK. But whether I'm in rainy Weymouth paying my own rail fare and eating chips or living the high life in Barbados on a sponsored trip, the task is the same

– to be fair and accurate. I ask myself these questions: would I recommend this holiday/place to friends? What are the plus and minus points? This may be the best job in the world, but it carries responsibilities: readers may spend time and big money on your advice.

Travel writing is not only about creativity, but organisation and time management. Before I go anywhere, I read brochures and websites, devising a rough schedule. I'm also keen to discover unusual or unsung places, so I chat to locals. That's how I found the bizarre giant model shark embedded in the roof of an Oxford house and a Barbados beach resort called Bath. Writing for local papers, such connections must be pursued. I went to Bath, took photos of rickety road signs by swaying palms and made it the start of my travel article. The opening of a piece is crucial: it must make an impact, especially for new writers out to hook a busy editor. Starts might involve a chat with an eccentric local, an event that sums up a place or something quirky – anything that makes people read on.

Many magazines use boxes of information: five attractions for families, where to eat etc. It's a case of putting in the legwork. Holidays may be about relaxation, but writing about them isn't. On the journey home, I rough out a plan of my piece, reorganizing the trip in my mind. I pick places to include, shuffle the order, allocate space and ponder links to help the flow. Sometimes, there is a theme or running joke. Ideally, I like my pieces to turn full circle.

Readers fall into three groups: people who might go, those who have been and armchair travellers who want you to take them with you. Whether cruising on the QE2, basking in a Caribbean beach sunset or exploring the Yorkshire Dales, be sure to tell a good story.

'These are my three top tips:

▶ Initially, be fully-focused on observing and experiencing a place; take photos later. Doing both together can mean you're distracted and miss things.

▶ Carry a little notebook to jot ideas and descriptions. Even a word or two will remind you later: *"town square, red roofs, artists, orange blossom scent."*

▶ When you think you have finished a piece, forget about it for a few days, then re-read it. The new 'freshness' will help you spot clumsy phrases, omissions or mistakes. '

4 – Over 50? Write about a Gap project

'Travel is fatal to prejudice, bigotry, and narrow-mindedness.'

~ Mark Twain

If you've chosen this module for your weekend, expect it to be inspiring. The Gap year – for the middle aged as well as teens – is one of the boom areas for travel writing. And there's a generation of baby-boomer readers out there longing to read what you write! Travel is probably one of their main interests.

Travel pieces for these Sixties survivors offer more writing opportunities than ever. Research tells us that 2,820,000 over-50s in the UK take three holidays a year, and spend £1,000 on each one. They're the biggest buyers of Gap travel – using a sabbatical, retirement, redundancy pay out or just letting out a mortgage-free house for a few months while they go abroad.

If you're in any doubt about the vitality of this so-called "grey market", look at its icons. Mick Jagger is 60-plus. So is Bob Dylan. Twiggy must be nearly there too. There are many Sixties stars who are still producing sell-out work, still attracting devoted fans, still delighting their fans of nearly half a century. Maybe Sir Mick isn't your typical reader, yet he represents that whole generation of baby- boomers who somehow haven't quite grown up – who still listen to serious rock 'n roll, still have a sense of humour, wear jeans, read newspapers – still read, in fact – and who remain interested in new ideas. Who's writing for them?

There's a whole world of freelance travel writing opportunities out there for the older-yet-not-old market. They've got some money (pensions, redundancy pay-offs, investments, inheritances, savings or just a house they can rent out), they want to travel, and now have the time to do it! And there just aren't enough writers catering for them!

So… *ideas?*

If you are in the "mature" age range yourself, that's a big plus! You'll know what interests you – you'll know that being older can make you more restless, give you more energy and more curiosity. You could incorporate the "oldie" angle into a travel piece, easily. Look at your own city or town with new eyes. Take a trip across it and pick out all the deals on offer for over-55s or over-60s. This will include cinema clubs, restaurant meals, cheap travel and courses offers, cut-price theatre tickets, free gallery and museum entry and shopping discounts. Write about the city for someone to whom it's new, an out-of-season tourist or tripper maybe. And they're quite likely to be older, maybe retired.

Take a look at local magazines. They may have unimaginative titles such as *Retired In Swindon* – and most of their advertisements may be for retirement properties and stairlifts – yet they'll be looking for quality copy that fits their reader exactly.

It's true that the lifestyles of baby boomers varies immensely: some 60-year-olds will be on second marriages and bringing up toddlers; some will be living in retirement communes while others will be embarking on new careers, university MA's in Creative Writing or starting their own small businesses.

Some will be caring for elderly parents while others go clubbing and windsurfing. It's a diverse market, yet their values and approach – forged in the quality decade of the Sixties – won't be so dissimilar. And remember, travel is near the top of their "happiness" list!

Target your market – Study magazines for the over-50s to see exactly what kind of reader they're aiming for. The cover will give you a good guideline – glossy and glam, down home and grannyish, cultured and serious. You can target your work accordingly.

Research the advertisements as well as the editorial features. Look at the main "point of view" read – is it sardonic, serious, witty, cynical, fun, earnest, outrageous?

> *Advertisements* – are they mainly for mobility aids and retirement home insurance or expensive help-you-sleep aromatic face creams? Are there many ads for film videos, music CDs and books from the Sixties era?

> *Editor's letter* – does it suggest readers are adventurous, or cheerful homebodies?

> *Readers' letters* – look at the values expressed: Top Shop fan with a pension maybe? Is there much chat along the lines of 'You'll

never guess what my grandchild came out with when she came for tea last week', or is it more, 'I took a scuba diving course on my 55th birthday'. Are there notes on the best boiler to invest in, or how to rent out your home for the winter while you live it up in a Cyprus beach apartment?

What's the ratio of emotional to practical features? Most magazines are looking at the "inner" reader and the "outer" reader; some magazines are almost entirely one or the other. You can adjust your travel ideas accordingly – the outer-focussed magazine goes for hearty travel (cycling round Germany, hiking in Tibet), while the "inner" one will welcome travel features that focus on relaxation, pampering and de-stressing on Red Sea spa breaks. Study the magazine carefully – where features go deeper into stress solutions, relationships, health, "fresh starts" –they they cater for the "inner" reader.

Is there a lonely hearts section? If there is, the magazine will welcome features on singles holidays, tips on taking trips alone, activity breaks and weekend holiday courses

60 – it's the new 40!

UNDERSTAND and empathise with your reader as you write. He or she doesn't feel any older – apparently, most of us stick at 37, in our heads

USE clear, plain English – no modern slang or slogans

DON'T apologise for being older

INCLUDE pictures – of yourself

USE humour and wit – your readers understand irony

SURPRISE readers – they've been around the block, some of them several times, and crave something new

PICK OUT budget travel deals, or tips on travelling in comfort for less

CUT OUT sentimentality, unless the magazine you're writing for is unashamedly sentimental and nostalgic

KEEP articles to a maximum of 1,300 words

MONEY, HEALTH, FOOD – all 50+ readers will have an interest in all these topics. Can you incorporate them into your travel piece…maybe an article on budget health food bars in Madrid, or a piece on five superb youth hostels for grown-ups, or a weekend on a fasting retreat in the UK?

5 travel writing ideas for the grey market

▶ Learn a language abroad – and write about it

▶ Find someone in their 50s or 60s who works in the travel industry – interview them

▶ Try a coach and sea journey to Europe

▶ Plan a Big Trip – India, Australia, South America? Awfully big adventures are popular with mobile late gappers

▶ Use that bus pass, and see how much you can get out of it in just one day! You can stop and start again, visit cafes, museums – all with no travel costs

Top 20 gaps

Here's a bumper list of travel and gap opportunities, any one of which would make an excellent piece – or pieces! They range from a few days to a few months.

One week or so?

Tour Europe by Bus…

Create your own trip, travel by coach and explore Europe on a Flexitrip Pass – the coaches travel through each destination every other day. Travel at your own pace, stay in each place as long as you like, with a notebook by your side. From £225

www.backpacker.co.uk

Study Yoga in Egypt…

An eight-day holiday in Dahab, an oasis on the Red Sea coast. Year-round warm water, daily yoga classes, a trip to Mount Sinai, camping with Bedouins in the desert and scuba diving. Keep a day-by-day diary. From £375.

Responsible Travel, tel 0870 0052 836, www.responsibletravel.com

Two weeks free?

Be a PR for the Terracotta Warriors...

English-speaking volunteers are needed to work at the museum of the famous Terracotta Warriors in the Chinese city of Xian. And after two weeks here, you can transfer to a traditional tea house, where you teach English and learn more about Chinese culture.

i-to-i, tel 0870 333 2332, www.i-to-i.com

Discover Navajo culture...

Travel with a Navajo guide through the red rocks, and spend evenings around the campfire watching traditional song and drum shows and munching tasty Navajo cooking. You'll be hiking through the Canyon de Chelly, one of the USA's best-kept secrets'. Eight days for £370.

Gap Adventures, Matrix Studios, 91 Peterborough Road, Fulham, London SW6 3BU, tel 0870 999 0144, www.gapadventures.com

Pick up Portuguese in Rio...

Long to visit Rio de Janeiro? Want to combine it with learning Portuguese? Classes are held near the beach, and you'll be in one of the world's most spectacular cities, with a double angle to write about. From two weeks, from £845.

Travellers Worldwide, 7 Mulberry Close, Ferring, West Sussex BN12 5HY, tel 01903 502595, www.travellersworldwide.com

Eat Vietnamese food...

You dine your way from Hanoi to Ho Chi Minh City, with tasting sessions and tips from experts. You'll learn more about Vietnamese history culture and culinary delights – and you'll get a marvellous food article to sell. Don't forget to take your camera, and to photograph all the food . . . £634 plus flights

Gap Adventures, tel 0870 999, 0144 www.gapadventures.com

Learn to tango...

You'll have a private tango teacher in Buenos Aires and in the first week, you'll see a tango show. Your trip also includes an open tango party each week and one group class per week. Make sure someone takes pictures of you, and aim the feature at any "brand new you" magazine such as *Woman & Home*, or a Sunday supplement of a newspaper. From two weeks, From £795.

Travellers Worldwide, tel 01903 502595.

Speak Italian in Florence...

Always wanted to speak Italian? It's one of the easier languages to pick up, and where better to try it than Florence? Its beauty will uplift you as you gain language skills and enjoy the delicious food and wine. Give your readers a daily tip on picking up Italian as well as travel info for holidays in one of Italy's most breathtaking cities. From £446

STA Travel, tel 0870 1630 026, www.statravel.co.uk

Work as a journalist in Romania...

You'll be on the English-language journal Brasov Visitor, working alongside Romanian journalists. So you'll get hands-on journo experience as well as experiencing life in mountainous Transylvania. Two weeks from £1,730.

Teaching & Projects Abroad, Aldsworth parade, Goring, Sussex BN12 4TX, tel 01903 708300, www.projects-abroad.co.uk

Be a French chalet chef...

Great skills here – you'll learn how to run a chalet, compose the right menus, get tips on kitchen management, health and safety – plus some basic language skills. I can think of several magazines that might love this – from *The Lady* to *Woman & Home*. Try the supermarket mags too, such as *Waitrose Food Illustrated*. Two weeks from £495.

Snow Crazy, tel 01342 302910, www.snowcrazy.co.uk

Explore the Land of the Thunder Dragon...

It's the world's last Mahayan Buddhist kingdom and has a breathtaking Himalayan travel setting. Join a walking holiday in the kingdom. Record plenty of detail – the country was never colonised and remains untouched by modernization, so it's a gift to the travel writer. From 14 days, from £1,730.

Responsible Travel, tel 0870 0052 836, www.responsibletravel.com

Got a month or more?

Study journalism in Ghana...

Based in the capital, Accra, you can choose from radio or print journalism. Gives you the chance to build a unique portfolio, and to write about this large West African state. From £1,445.

Teaching and Projects Abroad, tel 01903 708300, www.projects-abroad.co.uk

Learn Japanese...

Sandy beaches, buzzing city – Fukuoka is the largest city on Japan's Kyusha island. Lots of parkland and modern architecture – and lots to write about. Four-week courses from £1,210.

STA Travel, tel 0871 2300 040, www.statravel.co.uk

Live with nomads in Mongolia...

Live in a tent in the Gobi desert and teach English. A nomadic family will look after you and you'll help them produce diary products. A sensational experience to write about – take plenty of pictures and get some of you with your host family. From four weeks, from £1,495.

Teaching & Projects Abroad, tel 1903 708300, www.teaching-abroad.co.uk

Teach English to city guides in Vietnam...

You'll be teaching English to volunteers who offer tourists information. You'll help to boost the confidence of the volunteers – and you'll live and work in Ho Chi Minh City. Try this for magazines that love pieces on volunteering – they include *Good Housekeeping*, *Woman & Home*, *Saga* and *Yours*. Four to 12 weeks, from £918 plus flights.

i-to-i, tel 0870 333 2332, www.i-to-i.com

Be a Radio broadcaster...

A 24-hour radio station in Delhi, India, needs volunteers. You'll get experience of production, reporting, copywriting and newscasting. Work in all of the station's offices, or specialise in one department. Write your piece as a daily diary. Four to 12 weeks, from £889.

i-to-I UK, tel 0870 333 2332, www.i-to-i.com

Study art history in Italy...

If you've a small windfall to spend and love art, this is a gorgeous course lasting six weeks. Trips to Venice, Siena, Naples and Rome are included and you'll see some of the most awe-inspiring art in Italy. There's a daily tutorial, in a small group. Pick out some practical advice for your readers – both on the language and getting to know the group. You'll come home refreshed and inspired, with knowledge that will enhance your writing life. From £4,950.

www.arthistoryabroad.com

Work as a journalist in Moldova...

You'll shadow a local journalist in a newspaper office, then research your own features and interviews. You'll get time with the editor and you ought to keep your own journal – target your piece to the media or careers/travel section of any newspaper or magazine. From four weeks, £1,095.

Teaching & Projects Abroad, tel 01903 708300, www.teaching-abroad.co.uk

Take the Vodka Train...

Travel from Russia to China – there's a special deal for travellers aged 18 to 35. No regimented meal or sightseeing schedules, and you travel with local people, seeing the cities with local guides. You can choose from Trans-Mongolian, Trans-Siberian and the Moscow-St Petersburg Express. From £390.

Vodkatrain, Suite 207B, The Business Village, 3-9 Broomhill Road, London SW18 4JQ, tel 020 8877 7650, www.vodkatrain.com

Learn publishing...

Work as an editorial assistant at an award-winning charity organisation in New Delhi, India. More than 100 new titles are published every year, and the company works with leading publishing groups. From three to six months, from £1,850.

Gap Guru, 1st Floor, Bankside House, West Mills, Newbury, RG14 5HP, tel 0800 032 3350, www.gapguru.com

Good gap?

You've decided that a gap project would be good to write about. The best way to check out an organisation's integrity is to talk to someone who has recently returned from a project with it. All good charities will put you in touch with past volunteers. Quiz the returnees about the kind of people who volunteer, how much training there is, and who benefits from the project.

Be clear on what is included in the price. Volunteers usually pay for their own flights, insurance and visa. Many projects also ask for a contribution towards running costs. A gap project isn't free, and they don't pay you. Find out the total cost. It would be wise to have access to an emergency fund before you go.

Think about the climate. While a gap year in a tropical paradise sounds idyllic, remember that there's no such place as paradise, at least there isn't on this planet. It won't be the same as if you were on holiday. You'll be working, and you might have to deal on a daily basis with insects, intense heat and tummy upsets. An urban gap year in Europe may be a better option if you want to be more comfortable.

How much support is provided for you by the organisation overseeing the project? After the training period, it could well be that you meet difficulties. You may feel lonely and depressed, stressed, or find yourself short of cash. So think twice before you accept a project where there's no ongoing support.

On your volunteer project, will you have your own room? No matter how communal the project is, you may only be able to relax if you have at least a tiny space to call your own… and to write in. Dormitory or shared rooms don't work for us all!

Gap books, magazines and websites

The Career Break Book (Lonely Planet, £12.99)

Gap Travel Red Guide (Merricks Media, £8. 99)

How to Spend The Kids Inheritance (Annie Hulley Howtobooks, £12.99)

www.gapyearforgrownups.co.uk – trips from two months to two years – tel 01892 701881

Wanderlust magazine, www.wanderlust.co.uk, tel 01753 620426

i-to-i – volunteering overseas, www.i-to-i.com, tel 0870 333 2332

VSO – Voluntary Service Overseas, www.vso.org.uk

Plan UK, helping tsunami children – plan-uk.org

The Gap Year Show – for seniors as well as school-leavers – www.thegapyear-show.com

My 4th Golden Rule

Plan a Gap holiday you could write about. Send for the details, or print them from the website, now.

■ *Case study: How Jos did it*

Jos Simon, travel writer.

I was born and raised in Pwllheli on the Llŷn Peninsula in North Wales, where my father was head of one of the town's two primary schools. I studied in the 1960s at the London School of Economics (lots of fun – not much work!) and graduated (just) in 1967. A year later I married (to a Greek Cypriot) honeymooned in Athens and started teaching in Ipswich. Over the next 30 years, we built up our teaching careers, culminating in headships in South Yorkshire (my wife) and North Lincolnshire (me). Having both retired, we now live in Bawtry, a small market town nine miles south of Doncaster.

'In the mid-90s, I wrote and sent off an article with pictures to *Caravan Magazine*. It was about a short break my adult son and I had in Normandy. This was published (without warning from or contact with the editor) six months later. I realised that here was an activity which:

▶   Would provide, in the absence of kids who'd now grown up, a focus for future travels

▶   Combines all the things I enjoyed doing – writing, travelling, reading guidebooks, taking photographs

▶   I could continue, even expand, after retirement

Having already taught myself to touch type, on retirement I did two evening courses at Sheffield University – one on general journalism, the other specifically on travel writing.

I was now able to spend far more time on travelling and writing, and had numerous articles published in all of the main commercial caravan magazines.

A new young editor took over at *Practical Caravan*. She liked my work, and I became a major contributor – doing site reviews all over the country, and other long, commissioned pieces.

Keen to expand beyond the caravan magazine market, I approached *Greece* magazine – being married to a Greek, with family in Greece, and with experience of frequent tours of the country, it seemed a sensible progression. I began writing travel pieces for the magazine, largely about the Greek mainland.

I also write occasionally for other magazines in the Merricks stable. I particularly enjoy writing for *Holiday Villas* and *Holiday Cottages* magazines, because I end up going to places I wouldn't perhaps have thought of visiting myself.

I've joined the British Guild of Travel Writers, which is open to writers who have had 12 articles published in a year. Not only has the guild been an invaluable source of support and information, but the opportunities for networking (at the monthly meetings, the annual general meeting and on its website) help to counteract the isolation of being a travel writer based in the provinces. It was a recommendation from the chair of the guild that led to a commission to write a guidebook on Croatia for Frommer's.

My specialisms are:

▶ Greece, concentrating on the mainland (and especially Greek history and culture)

▶ Long distance touring in Europe

▶ Caravan and motor caravan touring

▶ Slightly off-the-beaten-track destinations in the United Kingdom and Western Europe.

I spend an average of 10–12 weeks a year actually travelling, depending on commissions and family holidays. It's difficult to estimate how much time I spend writing – if you include planning, researching, writing, contacting potential markets, putting pitches together, it takes up most of my mornings. Say three to four hours a day.

I take photographs, and since going digital, I always have my laptop with me so that I can download each day's pictures and clear the memory card for the next day. It must be very difficult to get articles accepted without usable pictures. I also find the camera useful for recording information, such as museum opening hours and memorial plaques.

For notes, I use a notebook, and some times a micro-recorder, but tend not to write anything day-by-day on the computer; I'm usually too shattered at the end of the day, fit for nothing more than a couple of drinks!

To do a typical piece (say 1,500 to 2,000 words) for a magazine, it would usually take me:

▶ Two days research/planning before the visit

▶ Two days writing the piece after the visit

▶ One day researching fact boxes, choosing and captioning pictures, and putting together the package (on CD and hard copy) to send to the editors

A 'day' is about four hours quality morning working-time, plus the odd couple of hours thinking time in the pub!

My top tips

1   Put together a small library of books about travel writing, plus some travel books. My favourite books about travel writing are *Travel Writing* by L. Peat O'Neil, the *Lonely Planet Guide to Travel Writing*, edited by Don George, and the *Writers Handbook Guide to Travel Writing*, edited by Barry Turner.

2   Join some of the many online organisations for travel writers – there are loads of them, though most are USA-based.

3   If you qualify (12 published pieces in a year, or one book), join the British Guild of Travel Writers (www.bgtw.org)

4   If you don't already take your own photographs, start. Modern digital SLR cameras are wonderfully easy to use – you don't have to get bogged down in technicalities (though the flexibility is there if you want it), as are programs such as Photoshop and its competitors. Not only have you got a lot more chance of getting articles accepted, your camera can also record information and scenes which you can describe when you're back home at your desk. I write my articles on a desk-top, with my laptop next to it displaying the photographs. It's a lot easier than writing everything down when you're in the field.

5   Develop a number of specialisms – you can't cover everything in the world, and it allows you to build up a relationship with the editors of the magazines that cover your areas of interest.

6   Include people in travel pieces. This means talking and asking questions, and jotting down the things people say. You should include people in pictures as well – a piece of advice that I often forget, having a penchant for buildings and landscapes. Some magazines like the author to be included in some of the pictures.

7   Get the opening paragraph or two written before continuing to the body of the article. I'm aware that this goes against the advice of a lot of travel writers, but I don't see how you can select the best anecdotes and events if you haven't established what the piece is going to be about.

8   Don't become obsessive about rates of pay. By and large, the more a sector of the magazine/newspaper industry pays for pieces, the harder it is to break into that market. So start at a realistic level, build up a body of work, and be patient. There's no harm in politely asking editors you are currently working for about a possible increase, but

you're more likely to boost your earnings by moving into a better paid sector of the market – from local to national papers, or from small-circulation to large-circulation magazines – than by perpetually moaning about what you're getting now.

My favourite travel writers are Paul Theroux, Jan Morris, Jonathan Raban and George Borrow.

5 – The practicals

'Every writer of travels should consider that, like all other authors, he undertakes either to instruct or please, or to mingle pleasure with instruction.'

~ Samuel Johnson

Now it's time to look at the bare bones of travel writing technique – all the practical how-to you need to write good travel magazine articles. For this module, you don't need to do anything; just read and absorb. Taking a few notes is helpful, or put yellow Post-It notes on pages you think you might want to go back to. You will probably want to get advice from it over and over again – this is your 'travel writing workbook' reference section.

Sit back in a comfortable chair with a cup of coffee, or even out in the garden if it's warm enough. This is a section to read and digest, but don't expect to remember all of it immediately. And don't be put off by seeing how much there is to learn. You will find that you pick up certain things quickly and remember them. Others take a little longer – you might have to check on other techniques several times before they stick. Don't worry – as long as you have this practical guide, and you keep using it, you won't go wrong.

Plotting the piece – intros, middles and endings

Apart from questions of style and syntax, the most troublesome aspect of travel writing for many novices is finding an answer to the fundamental question: where do I start?

It's a tough question because writing a feature article isn't like making a table. The wood and the decoration may vary enormously, but almost all of the tables I've ever seen have one flat surface held up by legs, normally no more than four. That's pretty much the iron law in the world of table design! When you are writing a travel feature, your choice of starting points can be terrifyingly vast. It could be the incident at the Greek Island taverna where the owner gave you a complimentary glass of retsina and then asked for your beautiful daughter's 'phone number; it could be your memory of the sun setting on the Italian island of Ischia, and on the last night of your holiday there; or the waitress in that New Hampshire diner who asked you about life these days 'back in the old country', and you responded, 'Oh, what old country might that be?'

It could be something that happened or something you saw or heard at any point in your trip – the start of it, the middle or the end – but it has to be something that is going to make an editor want to read on beyond that crucial first paragraph. That means it's very unlikely to be your account of checking in at Gatwick, or the two-hour take-off delay at Manchester, or little Terry's air sickness at 35,000ft just south of Madrid.

Bob Jenkins, a fine travel writer and a regular contributor to *Holiday Villas* and *Holiday Cottages* magazines, believes the starting point, the way in, to a feature, is the single most important challenge a writer must meet. He recalls a colleague telling him that you can't beat something like this:

> *I knew we were in trouble when the bartender collapsed.*

Here's a couple of mine:

> *"Yes, I think we'll survive!" said the monk sitting next to me sardonically as we bumped heavily down on the Athens runway, Greek passengers crossing themselves. That was the start of my impromptu monastery holiday.*

> *My low point at the new spa hotel in Halkidiki was dinner at the mocked-up taverna in the grounds. I was shoe-horned into a tiny table for three, between a couple clearly on their honeymoon. Escape wasn't easy – I had to eat something!*

Unless you are a natural – one of those rare writers who can sit down and bash out the right story in the right words in just the right order without any forethought – your first step should be to plot or map the content of your feature; just brief notes set out in descending order of importance. It could look something like this:

▶ Introduction: Village carnival or wedding/Invited to feast

▶ Middle: The beach/hills/walking trails/wildlife/cafes/food/local characters and customs

▶ Ending: Another village fiesta/you depart from quayside just as a boat unloads its cargo of café chairs, Coca Cola, Nescafe – and a coffin.

When you're happy with your map, the plan of what the feature should look like, start writing.

The way in – Sharp, stylish introductions – first paragraphs – are vital to the saleability of your articles. From them, an editor knows instantly whether you have something to say, and can say it well.

Here is an instant knock-out intro:

> *It's nearly midnight, almost 5 a.m. back home in Britain and I'm in a comedy club in an old ice hockey stadium, watching a stand-up comic who's half African-American, half French Canadian. I've just flown in on a direct flight from Heathrow and although I should be fast asleep, I'm wide-awake and wired. The comedians are speaking English, the bar staff are speaking French and I can't work out where on earth I am. Welcome to Montreal, the multi cultural metropolis where Europe and America collide.*
> *~ William Cook, The Guardian 2007*

Here's the opposite:

> *Paris overflows with flower stalls, crepe stalls and fine shopping. It's the perfect place for a weekend retail therapy trip. I decided to begin – after a delicious hotel breakfast of chocolate and croissants – in the Left Bank district.*

The first piece has real vitality – you can feel what the writer feels. You sense the thrill and the disorientation of the first few hours of the trip. You can hear the comedians, see the bar staff rushing about, feel that it's 5 in the morning for the writer. Even if you know nothing about Montreal, now you get a glimpse of it – it's coming closer.

And the second piece? Yes, Paris has flowers, crepes, croissants – yet the intro is lifeless, as though part of a hotel brochure. Paris remains a stereotype. My tip here – avoid "shopping" – focussed travel pieces. Readers want far more than that! In any case, most labels are global – and a lot of travellers like to think they travel "green", supporting local crafts and industries.

Burn the straw man!

Beware of the 'straw man' syndrome. This is where you begin a feature by suggesting a negative. You propose an idea and then go on to demolish it. Here's an example…

You may not have considered South Wales as a destination for your honeymoon. The weather is not always the best, the ambience is largely urban, and it doesn't have that magical honeymoon feel. Yet there are places you could go, such as the Gower Coast, and have as good a start to marriage as in the sunkissed Med.

Not that compelling, is it? Try this approach instead:

Keith and Ellie are toasting each other in champagne in an elegant waterside restaurant. They're going to order the fresh king prawns and raspberry tart with clotted cream. They could be on the French Riviera – but they're not. They're a few miles from Swansea. Yes, The Gower Coast in South Wales is the UK's newest and freshest honeymoon destination. The scenery is stunning, restaurants are as good as any in Mayfair and boutique hotels offer the perfect setting.

Even if the main body of the feature – the middle section – needs some editorial tinkering work, your aim must be to hook the editor with your intro. If it's inept, stodgy or downbeat – or just leaves the reader sighing a 'so what?' – he or she may not go to the trouble of reading the rest of it.

Exits – I like endings that sum up the story, that bring it to a graceful and satisfying close. It could take the reader back to the opening theme, or it could look to the future. A single, short summarizing sentence might be just enough. Here are five examples:

1   There are other ways to visit Spain, but staying in a palace has to be one of the most memorable.

2   If you decide to do the fabulous wine routes of Finger Lakes, print your own itinerary first. Make sure your chosen wine lodges have restaurants and book ahead – a liquid diet for 7 days isn't so great…

3   Castle X has always been one of the county's most charismatic mansions. As I drove away, I took a last look, drinking in its peculiar beauty.

4   If I'd stayed one more day, I'd have spent it entirely in the Benaki Museum.

5   We ate every meal outside, in the clear white sunlight of Venice in December. Just that pleasure justified the trip alone!

Intros and endings call for techniques that are not difficult to learn and apply. Go to a bookshop or library and pick a half a dozen books by the best travel writers. Study their techniques. Their writing styles will be different – perhaps strikingly so – but they'll be adhering to tried and tested principles.

Add your layers

The more professional your work, the better your chances of success. This means including panels – one or more – listing facts and information that may not fit comfortably into your main piece. They could be panels giving essential details for readers who want to know more about the resort, city or country you have visited and described.

They may want to know how to get there – by air, sea, rail or road? – and what the journeys might cost. How can they find out about accommodation? And the weather at different times of the year? Are visas needed? Are there good websites you can point them to?

A fact box could look like this:

Getting there – and around

Plane to Paris (website and typical cost of cheap flight, and of scheduled flight)

Train to Paris (website, costs, possible upgrades, what's included)

Hotel booking agency for Paris (website, range of prices)

Channel ferries (website, costs, what's included)

Metro costs in Paris (How much for a book of tickets? Any discounts for UK travellers?)

French Tourist Board (Phone, website)

Typical taxi costs, what do you tip?

Include these details and any extra ones you think would be useful.

For example, depending on city these could be

Typical price of pavement café coffee/glass of wine

Tour bus price

City's best/cheapest hotels, hostels

One or two major new attractions –

Zoo; Art Gallery; Park of statues; new opening of a palace.

Some magazine editors like to have more than one additional layer, because they're devices that help them to make their pages more attractive to readers. How can you please them? It's easy. Read through your article, pick out five of the most important points you've made – or ten sights that absolutely must been seen – and summarize each one of them in a short sentence. Like this…

No place like Rome – Five must-sees in the Eternal City

The Tokyo trail – Seven Tokyo treats for tourists

Sounds of Seville – Five Seville sounds you mustn't miss

There are still professional writers who believe that these layers are beneath them; that all that matters is their precious prose, and that if they're wanted, then someone else at the magazine can do them. But in many magazine offices, there isn't a someone else! Your chances of getting your work accepted will be much greater if the editor sees that it's complete – and that means sending it in complete with those fact boxes.

Neat writing tips

Your travel feature stands a much better chance of getting into print…

IF it conveys something about you, if there's a strong sense of your personality, and a sense of humour.

IF there's something new in it – something that only you have found. It could be a tiny café, a beach well off the beaten track, a unique shop or art gallery that's never been written about. The boulevards of Paris have been described time without number, along with the gondoliers of Venice and the canals of Amsterdam. Your job is to find that extra, new angle.

IF your writing style is good – that means writing simply with faultless grammar, careful use of adjectives and a determination to avoid travel brochure clichés.

IF you write concisely, never using ten words – when five will do the same job just as effectively. Try knocking the two short sentences of your opening paragraph – the intro – one. In most cases, the improvement will be 100 per cent.

IF you don't pepper your feature with foreign phrases or words when there are perfectly-formed English or American words that will suffice. English vocabulary is rich and vast: use it.

IF you resist the temptation to rely on your computer to produce readable copy. Computers do clever things, but they don't have brains – they cannot put text, or language, into context. When I wrote this chapter, my computer tried to: change 'your' to 'you're' several times; put commas in the wrong place; and changed correct spellings to incorrect ones. Computers have their place, but not where excellent English is concerned.

IF you write authoritatively and accurately. An editor told me about a feature submitted by a wannabe travel writer who'd placed Wexford in the west of Ireland. The editor's Irish geography wasn't too hot, so he checked on the map, where Wexford was clearly shown to be in the east. If something as simple as that was inaccurate, how many other mistakes were there in the piece? Could this writer's work be relied on, was the unavoidable question the editor had to ask himself.

Me, the travel editor

How did I become editor of a monthly glossy travel magazine? Surprisingly for some, perhaps, not by having done a university degree, a travel-writing course or even having worked as a freelance travel writer. It was in part a matter of luck: I had – and have – a passion for Greece, and I was working for a publisher who wanted to launch a magazine about Greece.

I've been editing magazines for about ten years, but my background and training was in newspaper journalism, and that's been invaluable because it means that I could think like a reader. Newspaper journalists and editors in Britain do not as a class have an enviable reputation, but they know – or used to know – what readers wanted. And as a travel magazine editor, I know they want to read about fellow travellers, not travel experts.

Readers love to be surprised, they want humour, and they enjoy hearing about other people's holiday joys and nightmares. Readers are holidaymakers or tourists who make the same mistakes and are inspired by the same sights and experiences. For most of us on holiday, it's warmth (or snow if skiing is your passion), interesting food, spectacular views and new friends.

A region's history can be interesting, but we don't necessarily focus on too much of it – unless we're historians and archaeologists. But we are interested in its modern culture, even if it's one of those Spanish resorts that tries as hard as possible to make British and German holidaymakers feel as much at home as possible.

From my newspaper training, I knew that what readers want is the personal – they want a strong sense of the writer's personality. They want to recognize something of their own hopes and fears in you and your writing – some affinity with their own anxieties and pleasures. There shouldn't be a distance between you and your reader – you're one and the same.

Tips from the reporter's room

My first purchase as a reporter was a 'contacts' book – just a chunky, sturdy address book in which I wrote down the contact details of everyone I talked to in the course of my work. You can do this, or keep a computer database, with e-mail, website and postal addresses, and phone numbers. Over the year, you build up an excellent network in your contacts book. If you buy the same kind of address book when that's filled, you'll collect a personal reference library that will be helpful again and again.

For travel features, there are several very easy things you can do to start yourself off:

▶   Go to a High Street travel agent and pick up all the brochures on "your" destination. Cut out all the pieces you need and keep them in a clear folder.

▶   Have a box or basket with coloured plastic folders, each one labelled with the country or destination.

▶   At the end of each day, save your work on CDs, and in hard copies in separate folders.

▶   Keep clippings of relevant information from newspapers and magazines.

▶   Buy a good atlas, and *Lonely Planet* or *Rough Guides* about the countries that interest you.

▶   Invest in a one-day language CD for the country you're going to write about

Keep things tidy! There's no doubt that a tidy desk helps when you are writing. Losing things – notes, essential leaflets, pictures – generates stress and wastes time. Here are some tips to inspire you to tidiness:

▶   Buy coloured paper clips not plain – they're much more fun to use.

▶   Buy postage stamps in blocks of 50.

▶   Keep pens and pencils in a pretty mug – one you really like, not an old chipped one!

▶   Decorate your office space with plants and a few fresh flowers.

▶   Look through www.viking-direct.co.uk (0800-424445) and see what little office extras you can buy cheaply. They deliver the next day, and orders over £30 are delivered free of charge.

▶   Tidy your office at the end of each writing day.

Simple subbing

One of the very first things I learned when I trained as a newspaper reporter was that after a feature had been written, it must be 'subbed', or sub-edited. It's a checking and revision process that ensures the article is fit for publication. Sub-editors would make sure the facts, spelling and grammar were correct, and that it had the right number of words to fit the space it was destined to fill. If the submitted article was too long, they would cut it. If the text was confusing, they would re-write it.

Magazines and newspapers used to employ large teams of sub-editors to do this work. But in recent years, cost-cutting has all but eliminated this safety barrier, and writers now are expected to handle the basic subbing themselves. There may be one multi-skilled sub-editor who can do a little work on your feature, but the less there is for him or her to do, the better. Editors have a preference for freelance writers whose work requires minimum revision.

These are the aims of subbing:

▶ To make your feature fit the space earmarked for it – and that could range from one page to as many as six. Read the articles in the magazine you are aiming at, and count the number of words in the published features. Ensure your feature – including the fact boxes – is not very much longer or shorter. There's no point in sending a 10,000-word travel feature to a magazine that never runs anything longer than 2,500.

▶ To ensure that everything that can be checked has been checked – phone numbers, websites, dates, place-name spellings and statistics.

▶ To ensure that there's nothing in the article that is a potential libel, or offensive. Don't use any of these: swear words; slang terms; jargon; foreign words or phrases; official-ese (English as used by politicians, civil servants and sometimes, travel brochures); words, even written jokingly, that would be hurtful or offensive to minority groups; words that could damage someone's reputation or livelihood – for example personal criticism of a travel agent or rep.

Your crash course in subbing

Subbing was traditionally done in red ink, so printers could quickly identify the corrections. To this day, subbing corrections are marked in red on the hard copy. You'll have equipped yourself with a few red pens this weekend, so you can do it the professional way, on your own work!

Obviously, subbing on screen is much quicker, and you can use the timesaving wordcount. But do not rely on your computer's spelling and punctuation checkers. These can be an unreliable guide through the quagmires of the English – and American! – language. So write and read through your article on screen, print it, read it again, mark further corrections in red and then make the amendments on screen. You will be looking for:

spelling mistakes

towns, cities, countries spelled differently within the same article

adjectives, nouns and verbs that you have repeated in the same sentence or paragraph

punctuation errors

over-long sentences

mixed-up tenses

verb confusion

inconsistency – have you used both £s and $s, miles and kilometres, e-mails and emails, St. Malo and Saint Malo?

Print out and check again. Keep doing this until there are no red marks. Do not expect to sub (or copy edit, as the Americans call it) your article to perfection in one go – I will do three or four read-throughs before I'm convinced an article is as perfect as I can get it. But when you've done all you can – yes, send it out!

Avoid getting too many opinions from family and friends on your travel feature. My view is that the more people you include for opinions on anything, the worse it gets! Writing can't be done by committee. When writing travel, your aim isn't to get the "received" view, or a view that includes everything everyone has said or thinks about the destination. This is your view and yours alone. So don't solicit too many opinions. I probably wouldn't ask for even one. That's why this weekend course is right for you – you won't be surrounded by people making 'helpful' suggestions.

Top tips

▶ Aim for succinct, 'clean' copy free of unnecessary adjectives and useless words such as however, actually, personally, notwithstanding.

▶ Keep it brief – the more economic you make each piece, the more gracefully it will read. Most copy can be cut by a third without losing any charm or information. Plain English is what you're aiming for – not flowery prose. Cut out any signs of snobbery, pomposity or boasting.

▶ Whether you're doing a 1,000-word piece, a reader's letter about a holiday, or a 100-word travel tip, check everything thoroughly. Use reference books, and a dictionary to confirm spellings. Do not ask anyone how to spell Thessaloniki; they could be wrong. Be accurate, always.

▶ Remember to answer all of the questions readers will be asking themselves: who, what, where, when, why and sometimes how? Don't leave readers confused.

▶ You don't have to keep thinking of ways to say 'said' – there are few better words for this purpose.

▶ Break up factbox info by using 'bullet points' – digestible pieces of information distinguished by an asterisk or other mark.

▶ Quotes from other travel writers, authors, poets, the Bible and so on must be accurate. Editors won't use your features again if you get them wrong!

▶ Also avoid using clichés in your work, especially these: clear blue skies; live the dream; quaint; picturesque; picture postcard perfect; chocolate box cottages; white sands; crystal clear water; Olde English; pretty as a picture; bustling town.

Sending it off

Most magazines want features – especially those sent by writers with whose work they're not familiar – sent to them on A4 paper. They don't want their e-mail in-box clogged up with submissions; they want to be able to read your work on paper, along with a brief covering letter telling them who you are and what the feature is about. Once you become a regular, you may be asked to send in work sight unseen by e-mail or on a disc.

At the bottom of each page of hard copy (that's old-fashioned paper, not text on a computer screen), put 'mf' (more following), and at the bottom of the final page, the word 'ends'. That way, it's clear when there's more to come, and when the piece is finished.

On the top of each page, on the right, put your surname, e-mail address and phone number – that's all. That way, on every page, your contact details are clear. And if a sheet of paper gets detached, it's easy for the editor to know where it comes from.

If, later on, an editor asks you to send him the feature by e-mail, send it as a plain Word attachment. Your work should be neatly arranged in paragraphs, but you don't need to format it in any way. Don't be tempted to use colours, highlights, boxes or borders. No formats and fancy fonts! Keep things simple.

Never send original documents and photographs, especially if they're not yours. Publications aren't liable if they're lost or damaged and, even if they were, that photograph of your grandmother, taken in 1916, can never be replaced.

Details, details!

Readers crave detail, as long as it's interesting and uncomplicated. Here's four ways to get more in:

1   Visual description is not the only way to create setting – notice sounds and smells as well. Use all the senses.

2   Look hard at your resort and find the colours that sum it up – in Greece, it's blue and white. In Venice, under a bright December sun, I had an impression of navy blue – the canals – and parchment and gold for the stone of the buildings.

3   Snatches of dialogue can strengthen the sense of travelling in a different culture . . . but never lampoon the way foreigners speak English. How good is your Spanish or Russian?

4   What is special about the modern culture of the destination? In Seville, I noticed the high grooming and polish of the city's young women: every one of them looked like a model. In New York, I reported that huge, first-class bookshops, both new and second-hand, are everywhere. This is a city that loves to read. Use modern culture as well as history.

Checklist

1 Get that factbox in – and get it right! Check the phone numbers, e-mail addresses and website addresses you have included. Do not just assume they're right because they were in a cutting or leaflet or travel brochure – they may have been keyed in wrongly.

2 If conversations with people – holiday home buyers in Majorca, perhaps, or hikers in Slovenia – are in your feature, ask people to spell out their names. Is it John or Jon? Sarah or Sara? Lisa or Liza? Anne or Ann? Roger or Rodger? It does matter, because people get annoyed when their names are spelt wrongly. Check. The worst thing is to have Lyn and Lynne when you are writing about the same person.

3 Check town and street spellings in local maps and guides. If places are spelt in several different ways – as they are in Greece – it doesn't matter which spelling you use, as long as you are consistent. Don't refer to Lesbos in one paragraph, then Lesvos in the next.

4 Information on websites can be reasonably usable, but will not compare with talking to an expert. Website information also goes out of date quickly, and was sometimes wrong to begin with. It's fine as a one reference source among many, but don't use it for material for an entire article.

5 Press cuttings – especially about travel– can be dangerous. You may find yourself repeating an inaccuracy or it may be that the place you mention has since closed or changed hands so that everything is different.

6 When you quote from a book – or suggest it as a useful read – give the title, author and publisher.

7 Reflect the style of the journal you are writing for. It's essential to read more than one copy, and to really think carefully about that style. Is it informal, serious, joky, factual? Is it geared at people under 30 or people over 60? At women only, at couples, or at a general audience? Because the words used will reflect the target readership. You'll be able to recognise the essential "style" only by reading a few copies.

8 When you start writing your feature, don't begin at the luggage carousel – start your piece in the middle of some action, such as a party, a church service, a meal, even an emergency of some kind.

9 Mesh in facts about the place with your own personality – how you felt when you were on the holiday.

10   Balance your piece; don't write a eulogy. There will be some low points; there always are!

11   Don't feel you have to be comprehensive. Be selective. Zoom in on one event, one journey, one adventure from the whole trip and focus on that. Then add subsidiary general paragraphs to build up the piece.

12   Don't use too many adjectives – say why you think a view is stunning.

My 5th Golden Rule

All your travel pieces must have a beginning, middle and end – and a factbox.

Case study: How John did it

John Shaw, travel writer and photographer specializing in green issues.

I was born in Manchester, and spent most of my early life in Middleton, a small town previously renowned for its cotton industry. I went to a comprehensive school near Oldham and, having left with a handful of O-levels, I went on to a further education college to take A-level courses.

My first job was as a civil servant specializing in national security work. After a few years I made the break and moved to the Far East to take up a post in the Hong Kong government. This lasted until 1992. Travelling around that part of Asia gave me a wealth of experience, and I became a freelance photographer submitting work to local publications. At first it was mostly of slides and film of wildlife and landscapes, but later it included architecture and commercial events.

Now I'm based in Manchester, where I'm a writer and photographer, depending on the offers I receive.

I got into writing in general and travel writing in particular when I realised that being just a photographer was restrictive, that I needed to produce the finished article. I am self-taught, although I have attended workshops run by the BBC in Manchester, and I read writing guides. I guess my style has evolved over the years. I started by adding a few words to my photographs and submitting the work as photo essays. I still like this style. Most editors wanted more information than you get in a short caption.

My first published work was for the *South China Morning Post*. It was a piece about a white dolphin that had been spotted off the coast of Hong Kong – a rare sighting in that part of the world. That was followed by photo essays about travel to nearby destinations such as Macau and Thailand.

I tend to specialize in environmental issues, particularly wildlife conservation work, although I will tackle any subject if I believe I can do it justice. Often, it's the self generated ideas that end up as published work. When I'm not writing articles, I do other photographic work, such as portraits and commercial commissions.

How much time I can spend traveling often comes down to cost and planning. It is very difficult to travel to a place, with all the expense that entails, take numerous photographs and write an article, and come home to find no-one wants it! I tend to plan two travel periods in a year. I come up with ideas of what would make a good article or photo essay, then research who might be interested in buying it. Sometimes I get a commitment from magazines, and guidance as to what they want, and try to fulfill that request. I would travel more extensively, but this would depend on commissions;

without them, it is very risky and expensive. My most recent project has been to Thailand to visit a tiger temple, for an article published in Singapore.

Once I have got all of the information and materials I need for an article, I draft a manuscript in one sitting. I come back to it for amendment and polishing, but usually a day or two is enough. But if it's a topic I am not familiar with, I could be writing on and off for a week. The most time-consuming work is researching your topic, plus writing the notes or taking the photographs that will be included in it

These are my tips for new travel writers:

▶ Adopt your own style; don't try to copy others. Although at times you will have to adhere to writing guidelines from an editor, be yourself nonetheless.

▶ Know your subject; there are no excuses for sloppy research and inaccuracies.

▶ Write about topics that interest you; if you are bored with the topic, it will be detected in your writing

▶ Give yourself enough time; don't do things at the last minute. We all have to meet deadlines, but where possible plan ahead.

▶ Write when you feel refreshed and in the right frame of mind; don't force it.

▶ Use local community events to practice your writing skills.

▶ Look out for writing workshops run as part of government initiatives, such as the BBC's skill seminars for beginners.

▶ Don't give up at the initial rejection. It may take time to get your work published, but persevere! I did, and it worked.

My favourite writers are:

Charles Dickens – wonderful reading, and such a variety of styles.

Patricia Cornwell – her knowledge of the subject is vast. Hers is a fictional world, but she makes it readable and interesting. ❜

6 – Writing about food

'Ask not what you can do for your country. Ask what's for lunch.'

~ Orson Welles

Travel is closely linked with food and wine. Let's admit it: they're two of the main reasons for having holidays and days out! Most of us love food. And we love reading about it. If you're a foodie (and this doesn't have to mean being an expert cook, or even doing much cooking at all) then you could write a food-related travel article this weekend.

It could be something very simple. I've written food pieces for different magazines, but never about expensive food or costly meals. My speciality has always been budget restaurants, hidden cafes, secret teashops, and bookshop bars – all the places I love. We all like treats in new places – crab sandwiches in Lyme Regis, a clotted cream tea in Dorchester, Bath buns in Bath, Welshcakes in Tenby, cider in Somerset, crepes and yet more cider in Normandy – every region, town and city has its specialities.

Sightseeing in a new city normally involves going out for lunch or dinner and stopping during the day for snacks and drinks. On a day out or a holiday, readers don't want to be disappointed, so the more original and cost-effective (as well as comfortable) your tips and ideas are, the better. Magazine editors appreciate the budget food/travel feature. I can't bear the restaurant review which concludes, "Our dinner for two came to a very reasonable £135." How many of us can afford that, or would want to spend it even if we could? Don't go there.

Magazines are always looking for articles that link travel with food and wine in a "non-textbook" way. The talented reader with a love of food and wine, and a flair for writing, is a gift.

There are many opportunities for getting into food and wine magazines, but first you must read them. In this market more than any other, it's essential to get as many of the magazines as you can and study their styles. If you already have writing talent – and you do! – then you're already ahead.

When I worked on a Marshall Cavendish food and wine partwork, I was surprised to find that none of the well known cookbook writers who supplied the recipes could actually write! All their work had to be edited, introductions written, tips and hints created from the raw material they'd sent in. And they were generously paid! That was a few years ago. That kind of editorial back-up would be considered an extravagance now, unless it's a mega-selling magazine that has a huge budget for ghosting the work of celebrity chefs. Most magazines want people with writing skills – not expert culinary talents – and an understanding of what readers desire: easy to read, clear and accurate copy, sprinkled here and there with a sense of humour.

You need a clear idea of the kind of reader each magazine aims to attract – and they do differ. Are they for the "organic, easy" young foodie, or the top-of-the- range convenience cook? Do they cater for the young couples who spend a lot of money on eating out but want fresh and easy recipes for the few evenings they stay in (*Olive*), or for the slightly more serious cook (*.delicious*)? Are you aiming at the middle-of-the-road cook – *Good Food* – or the earnest, knowledgeable and affluent wine drinker who reads *Decanter*? Are you preparing a piece for a local journal, with the focus more on the food event than on the food itself? You could even write something for a parish magazine on, for example, catering for a church supper or an Easter lunch, giving lots of ideas, tips and hints, rather than complicated recipes.

Dissect the mag!

How can you get beneath the skin of the magazine you are aiming at? You need to study it carefully, starting off by reading between the lines of the editor's letter – it's often here you'll find the key to the magazine.

He or she will always mention key features, especially those which put an emphasis on the magazine's editorial outlook. Some are green, wanting to be seen as eco-friendly. Many are geared for mums with small children, while others are for young couples whose disposable income has yet be seized by children. One magazine may feature organic food, another is keen on health foods and foods that aid health problems.

An issue of *Waitrose Food Illustrated* magazine had an editor's letter alongside a picture of rock climbing chef – and a feature on what top chefs do in their spare time. Readers are fascinated with every aspect of a chef's life – what they do when they're not slaving over simmering pans and shouting at their trainees. You could find local chefs who could provide you with a very sellable article. Don't forget that food features aren't just about food – they're about people in the business – growers, retailers and restaurant owners as well as chefs and kitchen staff.

Another magazine had a feature on what parents could do to improve children's meals – food-related pieces that would interest mums are ideal for a "family" women's magazine. What mothers want are ideas for speedy suppers, quick and healthy kid's lunches, slimming dinners and energy breakfasts. If you can find cooks, chefs and café managers at different destinations who know their subject, are happy to talk and can provide good photographs of them and their food – you can start selling food travel articles.

Wanted: New faces

All of the mainstream magazines carry ever-growing food and wine sections. And they look for new faces – they like fresh voices. Some of the all-too-familiar writers on the food pages are over-exposed, may be difficult to work with and expensive. The new, bright writer could, with a bit of luck, get a break with an editor who wants to change his or her menu.

Fast food champion

This story of an American writer called Duncan Hines shows how travel and food writing are linked – and how the piece doesn't have to be foodie, just entertaining and fresh.

He was the USA's champion diner-out; it was apparently a dull day when he failed to have six or more meals! But that's including morning coffee, afternoon nibbles and so on. When he was a young travelling salesman, he and his wife made an adventure of finding good food. Hines jotted down in a little book – a notebook he was never without – what he thought of the roadside places he liked. His friends asked him so many times for details that he published his list and gave them away as Christmas presents.

Friends of friends demanded copies. He published *Adventures in Good Eating*. Then came *Lodging For A Night*, and finally *Adventures in Good Cooking*. The books, updated through many editions, sold two million copies, putting them in the bestseller lists, after which Hines quit his sales job and devoted his entire time to them.

These are extracts from an article he wrote in 1947 for *The Saturday Evening Post* magazine. Every paragraph is a winner – clean, succinct and passionate. It's absolute proof of how resilient and simple good travel/food writing can be, with a style you could adopt today:

> *After many years of eating my way round the country, I have concluded that the principal reason for looking at the average menu is to see what to avoid.*
>
> *I never touch a Chef's Special, which is featured in hundreds of eating places that don't even have chefs.*
>
> *I never order a baked potato without inquiring when it was baked, because a warmed-over baked potato is about as edible as a gum eraser.*
>
> *Stale inedible foods are simple dynamite in anyone's stomach. From observing thousands of travellers in eating paces, I have concluded that the average American fails to get good food either because he doesn't know what good food is or because he is too timid to insist on good food. When he finally loses his appetite and patience, he bawls out the head waiter and sends the dish back to the kitchen. This is when I feel like going over to his table and saying: "Listen pal, just pay your bill and go somewhere else to eat. I have seen what they do in the kitchen to the food they bring back to cranky abusive customers."*
>
> *If you can't believe the menu and you can't send poor dishes back, how do you go about ordering a meal? I start by talking food with the waiter or waitress if he or she looks intelligent. I play safe by ordering ham and eggs. Not many cooks can spoil fried ham and the so-called chef who can disguise a neglected egg hasn't been born yet.*
>
> *I'm no gourmet and it doesn't take one to enjoy the adventure of discovering outstanding foods by the wayside. All I've had to do is be appreciative. I learned what brook trout can be like in Stillwater, Minnesota, where the guests at the inn net their own fish in a pool in the dining room, after which the waitress takes them to the kitchen. At The Toll House in Whitman, Massachusetts, I discovered chicken pie and a lemon-meringue pie with meringue four inches thick.*
>
> *We need more dining rooms with the leisurely tempo of California's Santa Maria Inn, a flower garden the year round, where if a patron admires a bouquet, Frank McCoy, the owner, may slip a cutting in a packet of seeds to be planted in her own garden.*

Or like the New England inn where your order is taken in the lounge and the table set with the first course upon it before you are invited to sit down.

Feel the food

Mention of refreshments used to be just a 'comfort stop' in travel writing, but now it's considered essential. Readers crave descriptions of food and they need detail. So don't just write . . .

"We stopped for a coffee."

Try . . .

"We stopped in the main square in Athens, Syntagma, for a fragrant cappuccino topped with whipped cream and sprinkled with dark chocolate flakes – even the flakes were organic, according to the menu. But best of all were the miniature pastries, which accompanied our drinks. They were tiny coffee eclairs, little strawberry tartlets and mini doughnuts lavishly dredged in icing sugar – each one just a mouthful. Syntagma is a bus terminal, tourist information centre and taxi rank all rolled into one. You couldn't enjoy more luxurious 'bus stop' refreshment anywhere in the world."

Read all about it!

So – are we obsessed by food and wine? I'll admit it: I am! I'm always thinking about food! I actually enjoy trips to Waitrose and other supermarkets. If the new issue of any of the supermarket free magazines is out, I'm very happy. Some magazines even have their own food writing competitions. But I love all of the food magazines and food sections in newspapers, and I have a collection of cookery books, including some very old ones. But my favourite cookery book isn't even a cookbook, it's an autobiography: *As Cooks Go* by Elizabeth Jordan (Faber & Faber, published in the 50s.)

The author was a freelance cook, and single mother, in the late 1940s and early 1950s, and her story is an entertaining account of her time at a cookery school in London, her freelance assignments and the jobs she had in hotels and restaurants. I love it for its period detail, which includes tips and hints on the recipes she dished up for clients. She talks about planning the recipes, buying the food, cooking in strange kitchens, dishing up and serving, successes and disasters. You might find it in a secondhand bookstore – I did – because it's out of print now. She moved around, and there are lots of travel details too.

Two other favourites – the ones I return to again and again – are *The Pauper's Cookbook* by Jocasta Innes and *Cooking in a Bedsitter* by Katherine Whitehorn. Books such as these can provide inspiration for a travel-related food feature. Vintage magazines often have food articles which may spark off a new idea for you. Look for them at jumble sales, market stalls and charity shops.

Build up your knowledge of international cuisine with books such as *Eating Out In Five Languages* (Bloomsbury Reference, £7.99) – it covers words, phrases and situations in English, French German Italian and Spanish. There's so much useful information for someone writing about food, from the "fork" ratings system in Italy to the typical times for meals in Germany, where breakfast begins at 6.30am, lunch starts at noon and is over by 2pm.

There's no copyright on ideas, or on inspiration. You can read other magazines and get ideas from them. Read new magazines. See if a relative has a stock of old magazines stored in an attic. You'll be amazed at how familiar some of the themes are, and by the new ideas they will ignite.

Cooking up ideas

▶   Lots of singles live in lofts or large, one-room spaces, often with a small galley kitchen at one end – a feature about cooking and entertaining in one of these would make a very good read. Call it " Cooking in the living room", or "Lofty cuisine".

▶   Are you living alone on a fixed income? What about a piece on catering for four friends for £12? That's in total, not each! Yes, it can be done. I've done it!

▶   How about something on budget eateries in your town or city? The best church cafes? Bookshop coffee bars?

▶   There could be a feature about the great kitchen utensils you've bought in charity and junk shops, and what you cooked with them.

▶   Write about your favourite take-away cafes. (Mine's on Pulteney Bridge in Bath. It sells the city's cheapest cappuccino, which I have to wash down a 50p piece of home-made chocolate shortbread.)

▶   If you're a student, write about your university city and its food, but from an undergraduate's point of view. List the cheap but good places, the supermarkets where you can get discount food at the end of the day, the speciality shops and the delis and the markets. Add to this a couple of your student supper recipes, attach a picture of yourself – or a group of you around the table – and your chances are pretty good.

▶ Suppose you learned to cook when you were 40 or 50, or when you retired? That would make a good feature. Be as candid as you can – offer your mistakes as well as your triumphs.

This kind of food writing – the personal mixed with the practical – is never out of fashion, and it's something you could do this weekend. First, you need to think of a theme, which is connected in some way with travel. It doesn't have to be set abroad.

Plus, you need a clear idea of the kind of magazine you'll be sending it to. And remember that it doesn't have to be a travel magazine – it could well be a food magazine publication.

Inspired? Get those notes down now!

Tips for local magazine features

▶ Suggest listings for cookery and wine courses; readers often want to pick up extra skills. Make sure you have a variety of prices from budget to prestige.

▶ Offer recipes a reader could do in a morning or an afternoon in your town, utilising some of the same ingredients.

▶ Children's cookery is an expanding area – anything in your neighbourhood? And there is cookery for men… and cooking for retirees… cooking for vegans.

▶ Do local restaurants host demonstrations? Why not go to one and write about it? That could be enough of a draw to attract visitors to your area

▶ Celebrity cooks sometimes appear in towns and cities as part of literary festivals, to talk about their latest books and cook up a demo. You might be lucky enough to get Jamie Oliver or Delia or even gorgeous Gordon – check out your local Waterstone's or Border's.

▶ Do your local museums have cafes? List the ones in your town or city and see if you can talk to one or two of the ladies who make the biscuits and bake the cakes. Museum visiting always seem to create an appetite for coffee and cakes.

▶ Do you live in a "cream tea" tourist area? Lucky you! Do your own personal guide to five of the best teashops. Give plenty of detail: how many strawberries on the plate, how many dollops of cream, clotted or double, the price and the features that make it different. This would make a great summer magazine read.

▶ Food and wine matching is another huge market. There's a shortage of new writers who can write well and in a lively fashion, yet include the basic practical details. Remember you need to offer labels, prices, suppliers and tasting notes.

Three can't-lose ideas

PICK a sum - £10, £20, £30 – and do a dinner party for friends on that budget. With lots of tips and hints, this is a winner for a local newspaper. Make sure you include a photograph of you and your guests, and the food.

CONTRAST the food for a family event, such as a wedding or anniversary, several decades apart. You'll need pictures of the original and pictures of the modern version. You'll need a few travel details about each location.

WRITE about a memorable meal you had abroad and recreate it at home, naming all of the ingredients and where they can be sourced here.

Seven trends in food writing

1   Vegetarian and organic cooking is in vogue – look for these outlets on your travels.

2   Rose wine and champagnes have become much more popular and affordable – think up recipes around them, visit a vineyard!

3   Celeb chefs are always good for an interview – do any live in your area? That's the sort of angle that could even bring visitors to your neighbourhood, so it's ideal for a travel piece.

4   Chocolate is big news, with specialist shops and cafes opening nationwide. Perhaps you could get an interview with a local chocolatier, who will give tips on creating recipes. Then expect chocoholics to invade your city armed with your piece!

5   Eastern Europe is opening up, with cheap flights to places like Talinn and Vilnius. Readers need tips and advice on foods to order / cafes to visit.

6   Why not do a piece just on museums, and their cafes? You could do this in the UK, or abroad.

7   Pavement cafes are now more evident in the UK – thankfully. Pick three or four in a city you visit, and make that your theme.

Crafty tips

▶   Use colloquial, breezy language, not serious catering-ese. You can whizz things in a blender, plonk things in the oven, blast them with cream or sugar – write the way you speak.

▶   Don't ignore your cooking mistakes – readers love to hear about them, and how you cooked your way out of them

▶   Wine is important now. For every dish you write about, pair it with a wine. Ask at Oddbins or Bottoms Up for ideas.

▶   Readers travel more, and supermarkets and delis stock produce from all over the world, so it's OK to use exotic ingredients and recipes.

▶   You can quote from other writer's cookbooks – a small extract of a few sentences is fair usage – but you should include the title, the author's name, and publisher.

▶   The more pictures you can offer to illustrate your feature, the better. Include some of you in an apron in the kitchen, at the table with friends and family, in the garden picking herbs – be imaginative.

▶   Can you establish a link with a local cookery class or school? It might offer readers a discount rate for a class if you mention it in your piece.

▶   Recipes must be accurate and clear, and to the same style throughout and format Use imperial measures with the metric equivalent in brackets, or the other way round – according to the magazine's style.

▶   Recipes should be double or even triple tested – do them and let someone else try them too, adding their comments.

▶   Visiting a place abroad – and you've got a *Lonely Planet* or *Rough Guide* with you? Try to find three recommendable cafes or restaurants that are not in the guides. When you write your travel article, you can then include original info.

Cash in on your travels

Food and wine holidays are popular – and they're a gift for a writer.

Write about…

A holiday visiting wineries, or a wine cruise or tour

A cookery holiday here or abroad

One day spent on a specialist cooking course – seafood, for example

A day or weekend learning to taste wine

A cocktails workshop, or a coffee making seminar

A special skill you learn on a weekend or day course – could be baking bread, icing cakes, Christmas cookery, puddings, children's cookery

Learning your way around the cheese boards of France

A cruise – Stelios does them now; easyCruises! – with cookery demos on board

Talk to them

Maybe you'd prefer to interview and write about foodie people? Think about these – they could form the basis for a travel/food feature about your village, town or city.

AN award-winning landlady or B&B owner of the year.

SOMEONE who runs a specialist cheese shop or exceptional wine bar.

MARKET TRADERS with a high reputation – could be in deli, cheese, ground coffee, breads or sweets.

HOSPITALITY administrator for your local council.

FARMERS' MARKET stallholders.

WEDDING VENUE organisers – could be on boats, at spas, racecourses – any unusual venue. How do they do their food?

WOMEN'S INSTITUTE cooks – they're always excellent and love to talk about their work. They also know the area they live in – great for travel tips.

SLIMMING and health gurus who can suggest diets and recipes… and give a discount for holidaymakers in your town.

What's good where you are?

What is your city or town famous for? Special sausages, Scottish smoked salmon, West Country cream, cider or mead, Welshcakes or bara brith, some kind of beer or wine, Caerphilly or Leicester cheese, Billingsgate or Brighton prawns, Whitby fish and chips, local bread or Bath buns, jam or chutney, even meat – Welsh lamb or Norfolk turkey? All of these give you a travel/food angle… mine them!

Be practical

As you travel about, always keep a small notebook and plenty of pens in your bag.

Invest in a special small file for restaurant cards with their name and contact info on – you can buy these special books from Paperchase. Collect cards abroad and file them when you get home. Buy a recipe notebook, write down new ones, and your own, with comments, and keep a record ready for when you write an article.

If you are combining a local food/travel theme, collect leaflets and tourist info and keep them in a small polythene folder in your bag. You can buy A5 coloured folders from Rymans. Leaflets kept loose tend to get lost! Money matters; when you buy food products or ingredients, keep a note of the prices.

Don't get carried away just by the food! You must set your piece firmly in a travel context. When you've written it, check that you have included detail about the destination as well as the food. Make sure you have tourist information office contact details in case readers want to visit – some will!

Food marketing

Marketing your work is important, especially locally. I liked the application I had from a food writer – she enclosed with her work examples a well-wrapped biscuit she'd made! I also had some miniature cakes sent to me with cuttings, when I edited a celebration cake magazine. If you are marketing and can deliver by hand, you could include a few sweets, a small pot of home-made jam, chutney or cheese bread with your writing samples. The value of this kind of marketing is that editors remember you – especially if the food is edible – and your originality and confidence shines through.

Think of having business cards with a relevant theme, such as a sketch of a plate of fish and chips, a glass of wine or a cake. Try www.vistaprint.co.uk – cards are free.

Take easy, achievable courses yourself – perhaps a wine diploma, a cookery workshop or short course, or a travel and cookery holiday. Put these in your writing CV, as it gives you more authority. And flag up prizes – for example, WI prizes, or any competition where your cookery skills shone. Never be shy of mentioning your success. Always send a small picture of yourself in a food-related setting with your marketing letters.

There are so many angles, so many possibilities in food and travel writing that, if this is your interest, try first to exploit it locally. Write to the newspapers, magazines and journals published in your area, using my tips. You're not likely to be offered huge, or even any, fees, but you will achieve profile, be invited to cookery courses and events, sent press releases and samples. Maybe you could end up making a book from your articles… that often happens to people who write about food, expert or not.

Get in the mood!

You can help your food and wine writing along by:

BREWING Italian or French coffee and drinking it at your desk – the aroma will be atmospheric of the country

EATING snacks and meals of the country when you work – could be croissants, pasta, Greek yoghurt, Spanish cheese or paella, Greek salad

PLAYING the right music – Rough Guide does a line of world music CDs with offerings from Greece, Turkey, Italy etc.

WEARING perfume or using bath oil from a French, Greek, Italian or other beauty products company – try www.korres.com for Greek ones.

How to compete

Magazines – travel food and mainstream – run food writing competitions from time to time, so it's good to have something ready to enter when you spot them.

Here's what the judges want:

Something different – a culinary disaster, a meal abroad that went wrong, a romantic meal in Venice that turned out not to be – something that isn't a cliché

Anything with a little humour or irony

A feature that demonstrates resourcefulness with food – maybe an amazing beach picnic, a dinner party without electricity, entertaining in a cave in Crete

Your entry will go down well if it includes listings of good recommendations for readers – anything from a one-table pavement café in Naples to a glamorous beach hotel in the Peloppenese.

Ready, steady, write!

All set to start your food piece now?

DECIDE which magazines you are aiming at

THINK in terms of 800 – 1,200 words

DECIDE on your "food" theme – say vegetarian bistros, or bookshops with their own cafes? Church coffee bars, wine shops with tasting sofas, training restaurants, chocolate cafes, tapas bars, wholefood bistros…

DECIDE on your "travel" theme – say Paris for the vegetarian bistros (look up some listings first in travel guides, then find one or two more) and Oxford for the bookshop cafes – they'll be in Borders, Waterstones, maybe one or two church and academic bookstores, Bath for the chocolate cafes, Athens for the wholefood bistros, Durham City for church/cathedral cafes, New York State for the wineries…the list goes on!

PLOT a structure that allows you to link them. This could be "48 hours" in a city, or four meals under £10 – something like that. You can visit more, but then select your "best" places to write about. Keep masses of notes and pick up as many business cards, menus, leaflets, and brochures as you can. The worst thing is to visit the ideal place to write about – then come away without a full address or phone number!

SCHEME your food hints and tips into your piece – get them down first when you write. For example, little tips on making vegetarian snacks – gleaned from your visit – or four tips on what's best to order when reading a new book in a bookshop (i.e. NOT jam doughnuts or spaghetti bolognese!)

PLAN your factbox and research the listings – with the help of all your notes and leaflets. The main thing is, phone number, address and possibly opening times for each place you visit.

As you build this up on your screen, you'll see that a piece is already emerging – and you haven't had to do any real writing yet. Once you've got the bread and butter stuff in, then you can get down to your main course!

My 6th Golden Rule

Sell travel articles on food by writing about budget eats, or writing about cookery holidays.

■ Case study: How Marie did it

Marie Barbieri was the winner of Greece magazine's first travel writing competition. She has written a selection of food/travel features, including pieces on vegetarian restaurants in Greece and the country's ten best cafes.

I grew up in London and left school at 16. My ambition was to become an actress or dancer, but coming from a poor background and without A-levels, I went straight into shop work.

At 20, I lived and worked in Australia for one year and developed an insatiable addiction to travelling and photography. I returned home with 3,500 photos and never comfortably settled back in England; I was always itching to work the world again. I saved for five years and after another one-year round-the- world-trip, I went to De Montfort University in Bedford to do a Higher National Diploma in Performing Arts, followed by a drama degree at Exeter University. I planned to teach with this, and embarked on a Postgraduate Certificate in Education, but became ill on my course, which I had to leave. Complementary therapies were my recovery. Thoroughly inspired, I trained as a complementary therapist and I still run my own therapy practice today. I wanted to write about my subject, and began a Writers Bureau course.

After joining Writers Bureau, I had features on health topics published, and some articles in my local county magazine, but I was desperate to reach the travel writing section of my course. *Greece* magazine ran a travel-writing competition and as the island I love most in Greece is Mykonos, I immediately set to work writing about a trip I'd taken there – a trip that had changed my life. I found the experience of crafting it inspirational and enlightening. Transferring the passion I have for Mykonos and its people into words felt natural; I knew I had found my niche. Winning first prize was unexpected and thrilling, and my thirst for travel-writing has never ceased.

Greece commissioned my first travel piece, The Gold and Silver Islands. This was an exciting challenge, as I knew nothing about jewellery. I quickly realised how important my ability to research speedily and effectively to a deadline was. This held me in good stead when I was asked to do a piece on Greece's ten best cafes, followed by a feature about vegetarian restaurants in Greece. I had to research recipes and talk to chefs and restaurant owners – and get barmen to part with their best cocktail recipes!

Although I still write about health and complementary therapies, my passion is travel writing and photography, specialising in Australia, Greece and Italy. I spend about 12 weeks a year travelling and writing.

I take my laptop, a back-up hard drive and my precious digital SLR camera – and a back-up camera just in case. I always take my own photographs. They're not merely an accompaniment to my words; they're of equal importance. I work as hard on images as I do on text, and I gain equal personal satisfaction from both.

How long it takes to write and finish features depends on how much research is involved and if there are interviewees. Because I am often juggling articles, waiting for replies, photographs from interviewees etc, they often come together in stages. If I am writing an article straight, it may take approximately one week. But I'm a perfectionist and pedantic in every way, so I often spend longer than I should proof-reading and editing. And I adore it!

These are my tips for new travel writers:

▶   Analyse your market. Know the magazine you are targeting inside-out.

▶   Never give up when rejections come in. Read the feedback editors give you and re-work your pieces – critical feedback (positive and negative) from editors is crucial to your success.

▶   When travelling, get out there and really explore. Talk to real people – this opens up valuable opportunities and even lasting friendships.

▶   Have an immaculate filing system for all of your article outlines sent to magazines, completed submissions, invoices sent and your expenses and mileage, which you will need for your self-assessment tax-return.

▶   Protect your photographic archives. Always caption your digital photographs while on your travels, otherwise you may forget where some of them were taken. Make back-up copies; once that hard-drive/ memory card packs up, so do your commissions!

My favourite writer is Bill Bryson – a likely choice, but I find his seamless blend of research and humour irresistible.

My weblink is www.travelwriters.com/mariebarbieri '

7 – Property matters

*'Go confidently in the direction of your dreams.
Live the life you have imagined.'*
~ Henry David Thoreau

*'I couldn't settle in Italy – it was like living in a
foreign country.'*
~ Ian Rush, Welsh footballer on moving to Turin

Can you guess what one of the major topics for travel magazines is? It's writing about your place in the sun – and the place in the sun you wished you had. And to write about them, you could be someone who's turned that place in the sun dream into a reality, or a specialist working in the travel or overseas property industries. There are plenty of slots for people within these businesses who can offer magazines Question & Answer features (known as Q&As), a point of view column on aspects of travel or buying homes abroad or perhaps their own living-in-the sun diaries.

It's estimated that 800,000 (and rising) British households own a house or apartment overseas, with Spain, France, Italy, Florida, Cyprus and, increasingly, Greece and Turkey, being the most favoured places in the sun. Many see it as the most sensible and enjoyable way to spend a redundancy or pension package, and with cheap flights and the ease of moving money across national frontiers, it's so much easier to travel and buy in a foreign country. And to write about it!

Look in Borders, WH Smith or supermarkets, and you'll see plenty of travel magazines which are well written, interesting and with a strong property focus. They showcase properties for sale, have interviews with and diaries by people who have bought homes abroad, and carry columns of buying and financial advice from experts.

If you own a property in the sun, or are searching for one, it's likely that you also have the desire to write about your experiences. The fragrance of fruit trees growing in your garden, the scent of geraniums on the path, the aromas of garlic, herbs and lemon when taverna meals are being put together, the strangeness and yet the familiarity of being abroad in a country you love, the disasters as well as delights – perhaps you long to put these impressions down in black and white, and see them published.

Maybe you are working in the overseas property or travel business – and would like to see your company mentioned in magazines? You've seen features and columns by colleagues in the biz – and wondered just how they manage to do it? There's no doubt that readers take a great deal of notice of informative features which are in the editorial – not the advertising section – of a magazine.

So how to make the first move, your first pitch? In your letter to the editor, put the magazine and the reader first – not your company. Don't write it as if you were drafting an advertisement for your company. Your writing must be so good that the editor can tell, from reading it, just what kind of writer you'd be.

This approach is one that could work…

Dear Diana,

I'm a great fan of your magazine, which I feel perfectly represents all that's best about France. We have a home there, near Nice, where we aim to spend six weeks a year for family holidays.

We have a small travel and property company specialising in off-the-beaten-track holidays in France, often involving wine tastings and cookery classes, and re-location services for people looking for homes in southern France. If these were of any interest to you, I'd be happy to let you have more details. If you ever needed a question and answer column or a feature on these and related topics – with tips for readers on making the most of such holidays and living in France – I would be delighted to offer a sample.

There would, obviously be no cost to you, if our company's contact details were to be included. Or there might be something else you are looking for, so do please let me know. We have a good library of high-resolution pictures which could be used to illustrate the features.

This pitch is unlikely to get very far…

> *Dear Diana,*
>
> *I have been advertising in your magazine for the past ten months – and think I deserve some free publicity! I'm not very impressed with the property editorial content, and feel I could offer something far more authoritative. Could you let me know what your fee would be for material from our property company, which is based in Brittany. I can give you property hotspots and pictures to go with them. I look forward to hearing from you soon.*

In my opinion…

If you own a property or travel company – or you have that place in the sun and want to write about it – kickstart your life as a published magazine writer with a short opinion piece that's something to do with travel or living abroad. All you need is that opinion – a point of view you can express clearly and that will interest others.

As more people get their hard news from television, radio and the internet, magazines – and newspapers – are publishing more opinion and comment features than ever before. In many ways, the viewpoint article is once again the lifeblood of magazines and newspapers, just as it was when Gutenberg's printing press gave us the first pamphlets and newsletters.

Supermarket magazines publish opinion features, too. Have a look at the travel supplements in daily and Sunday newspapers; they want opinions on destinations and travel from readers. They want readers to write as much of the content as possible! Anyone with a flair for words has a huge advantage. It's simply a matter of writing in a logical, direct and honest way. The cleverest argument, presented incoherently, will have no chance of being published.

For a property or travel company writer, the opinion piece is a gift. You can write it from your desk. You need no interviewees – it's just your opinion based on your professional experience, so extensive research isn't needed. Your writing skills are all you need. Think pieces are short – they need be no more than 350 words – and certainly no longer than 750.

Finding your topic

Pick a subject you feel strongly about. Or annoyed or concerned about. It could be about something very topical, something in the news this week, that has excited your interest. It needn't be negative. You might want to write in support of airlines charging more for check-in luggage… the case for travelling light, with brief tips on how to do it.

There's no shortage of travel and overseas property topics. Think about some of these:

▶   Is buying a second home in Bulgaria really a wise move?

▶   Buying in Europe – should your mortgage be in £s or €s?

▶   What's best – off-plan or ready-built?

▶   Our French gite horror story

▶   Living with the Italians

▶   What's Spanish for 'quick, I need a plumber'?

▶   The lure, and the downsides, of exotic and unfamiliar destinations

▶   Single supplements for lone hotel guests

▶   DIY internet booking v travel agents

▶   Independent travel v groups

▶   Women-only holidays

▶   Climate change and carbon footprints

▶   How I found my Algarve retreat

▶   Settling in Cyprus

▶   Florida – we live the American dream

▶   Protecting your pension in Portugal

▶   Best insurance deals for homes in the sun

Commandments

Here are my Eight Commandments for the opinion piece:

1   Your thoughts can't be thrown down randomly, however angry or passionate you feel about the topic. Like any other piece of journalism, the comment piece must be structured clearly and logically, enabling the reader to follow you effortlessly and enjoyably from one paragraph to the next. The reader will no more persevere through a jumble of seemingly unconnected statements and assertions than he or she would listen to a drunk ranting on a street corner.

2   Decide what you want to say – what your main point is – before you start writing. Limit yourself to just one principal point, and no more than two or three subsidiary ones – not 15. You're aiming for a short comment, not an essay for a degree course.

3   Draft a rough outline first – a sort of map of the piece, starting off your introduction and your major point and following up with one or two minor ones. When you have your plan, start writing, with a couple of paragraphs on each point, keeping strictly to your outline. Conclude with a summing-up sentence. Make sure it's not too long (if it is, cut it), and polish. Now it's written!

4   If your opinion is based on facts, make sure they're accurate. If you're using statistics to support your opinion, attribute them and keep the original information handy, in case an editor wants to be assured that you haven't just made them up!

5   Be succinct – do not use ten words when the same job can be done just as well with five better chosen ones.

6   Don't be pompous.

7   Choose the opening words with extra care – it's the sentence that will grab the reader's interest, or send them off to another article – or sleep!

8   Don't go in for anger or personal abuse (although gentle ridicule is OK) – and get a basic grasp of the law of libel. If you say someone is a liar, or a crook – or if you say anything that could damage his or her reputation – you and the magazine could face legal action that could result in large fines and even bigger legal bills unless you can prove that what you've written is true or fair comment. Most libel cases are lost by writers and publishers!

Suzi's 8 superb tips

Suzi Stembridge has been an air hostess (that's what they were known as in 1960, when she worked on the first charter flights out of Southend airport), a holiday brochure writer and the owner of two travel companies specialising in Greek vacations. She's also a travel writer.

Suzie and her journalist husband live in Yorkshire, but they've built a house in the Peloponnese, where she plans to finish writing an historical novel about Greece.

These are her writing tips for people in the travel and overseas property business:

1   Specialise, and learn as much as you can about your subject.

2   Buy the magazine or newspaper you want to write for, and learn as much as you can about the people who run it. Read and digest the articles written by its top travel writers.

3   Seek the quirky angle to sell your story; journalists are always on the lookout for the topic which lifts a story above the mundane.

4   Ensure your facts and spelling are accurate. Do not rely on spellcheckers – they're unable to pick up wrong words – he instead of she, it's for its, there for their, for instead of four!)

5   Keep yourself in the limelight. Journalists and editors are only ordinary people, so never feel that you should be obsequious or that you should not bother them. Go to conferences or literary festivals where you will meet such people, and introduce yourself. Failing that, find out an editor's name and write to him or her, addressing your letter or e-mail to them personally.

6   With all I have said about putting yourself forward, it is also important not to be too pushy, and to always be polite.

7   Protect your work by using reputable publishers and copyright.

8   Never send unsolicited work on a disc or by e-mail. It's better to send a hard copy by snail mail; most publishers prefer this at first.

You, the agony aunt!

Next step – a magazine would like you to write a Q&A feature about overseas property or travel, or a regular opinion column.

5 ways to keep the relationship sweet

1   Don't ask for a written agreement or contract (since, anyway, magazines and newspapers can't guarantee publication). These unpaid arrangements work only when flexible – allow them to be. You're providing free editorial and the magazine is giving you valuable publicity space, free. It's not a bad deal.

2   Always present copy the way magazines request it: don't be tempted to colour up your copy, use fancy fonts or formats or embed pictures in your Word files. Not got Word? Then get it! It's the industry standard. Send material in the way they want it: it may be pictures to one e-mail address, copy to another.

3   Send either clear prints or digital pictures set at a high resolution – a minimum of 300dpi. Don't imagine that because a picture looks huge on your computer screen, it really is big; when printed on glossy paper, it could be the size of a postage stamp. You may be asked to send pictures on disc; they're easier to organise that way.

4   Don't ask to check the copy, or arrange for anyone else to. Don't promise the people you mention that they will get the opportunity to vet the copy.

5   Whatever you're writing – an opinion column, a Q&A feature or case studies, try to get two issues ahead. The editor will love you!

Picture points

Pictures are a must if you're writing a case study about people who have bought a home in the sun, or about your own holiday home. Have you ever seen a property magazine, or a newspaper feature, without pictures?

But most of the pictures you see in these magazines are dull; the houses may be spectacular, but after a while one villa in the Med begins to look much like all the rest because the photographs are featureless. Try if you can to get people into your pictures.

continues...

Picture points (continued)

If your picture is of a new property, have someone sitting by the door - a child maybe. If it's the kitchen, lay up for a meal and have someone in there drinking a glass of wine. Put flowers on tables and casseroles on stoves. Think the pool and sun terrace are photogenic? They'd be even better if there were people in the pool and trying the sunbeds for size.

Journalists are many things, but few have the telepathic powers needed to write captions for pictures that are sent without brief details about what, or who, is in the photo.

Number your pictures (Paphos 1, Orlando 4 etc) and include in the picture package sent by e-mail or on a disc a Word file list that should look something like this:

Paphos 1 – Our villa in Paphos, exterior view.
Paphos 2 – Villa kitchen.
Paphos 3 – Lizzie shopping at the local market.
Paphos 4 – Our children in the pool.
Paphos 5 – Nico's Taverna, our favourite.
Paphos 6 – Lizzie by the pool.

Be the one they ask back...

Be generous with your advice and insider tips – give more than you need. For example, you can...

OFFER an e-mail service to readers – answer their questions on property and travel. Each e-mail is a marketing opportunity for you!

OFFER to be a resident expert on the magazine's phone-in day. From your own phone, with readers calling you, you can give a personal clinic. This has worked brilliantly for me on several occasions.

MAKE a DVD or CD which the magazine might give away to readers. Normally this comes at a price, but if you've been working well with them, there's sure to be potential for a good discount.

FAQs

If I advertise in a magazine, will it help me to get "free" editorial?

It helps you to build up a relationship. You're in a much better position to talk or write to the editor. You have a way in, but never expect that you'll have an automatic right to editorial. Build up a friendship.

How does a magazine editor choose which business people will contribute to the magazine as writers?

Always by the way they do their own marketing – good pictures, clear smiling pictures of themselves and their own staff, eagerness to submit a "sample" column, reliability, good computer skills (if they can send high res pictures and plain Word text document with no fancy formatting) a sense of humour and a sensitive and polite approach.

If I write a piece for a magazine, can I mention the name and contact details of my business?

Yes, in a separate section at the front of the feature. Give your job title, the company's name, a brief description of the business, telephone number and e-mail and website addresses.

Will the magazine let me have a copy of the edited piece before it's published, so that I can check it?

Yes, most will, provided they have your copy in good time.

Can I ensure that my piece goes next or near to my advertisement?

You can't ensure it, but you can certainly ask.

Will I be paid for my editorial contribution?

No – you are getting free publicity.

Will the magazine's staff help me with polishing the feature?

What staff? There will be a little bit of polishing needed, and one or two minor text changes may be needed to make sure it fits the magazine's style – is it miles or kilometers, £, $ or €, organise or organize, Paphos of Pafos, US or USA? – but editors are unlikely to have many people helping. The more polished your work already is, the better your chances of a column which sticks.

If I do get a column, how long will I be able to keep it for?

Provided all goes well, expect it to last six months to a year. I generally change columnists every year, yet a really good one can be "re-invented" and take over a different column after a break. I've done this several times.

How important are the deadlines – is there a bit of leeway if I have business matters to deal with?

Magazine deadlines are crucial to its publishing business, so they can't be toyed with. If you want to write for the magazine and have the free publicity it's giving you, meet the deadlines.

Making your PR pay

Strong writing ability is high on the list of must-haves for public relations people. Is writing press releases part of your job? The wastepaper bins in magazine and newspaper offices are deep. They need to be, because 95 per cent of the press releases editors get are flung into them. And sending a badly-written press release by e-mail makes no difference. The delete button on an editor's keyboard is never under-worked.

How can you make your press release, on travel or property overseas, stand out?

It's possible to write it so seamlessly that it slots into the magazine with barely a change. Here's how:

READ the magazine carefully for style. Is it matter of fact, enthusiastic, witty, practical or bossy? Your tone must match the magazine's.

SIZE matters. Check the word count of articles and news snippets. Match your length to theirs.

AVOID making your piece look like an advertisement. It needs to read like a magazine article, yet containing all the necessary facts.

WRITE an attention-grabbing introduction, but don't go way over the top. If it strikes an editor as being silly, juvenile or just far-fetched, your press release will be binned – or e-binned – largely unread.

My 7th Golden Rule

You will succeed in property writing if you follow the editor's agenda, not your own. Great benefits will follow.

■ *Case study: How John did it*

John Batty, travel writer and owner of Aegean Blue, Greek property specialists.

'I was born and brought up in Stockport, where I attended the local grammar school and started work in a bank. It was intended to be a temporary job while I decided what I wanted to do with my life, but I stayed in banking for more than 30 years! Six of those years were spent in Greece and, as they say, one thing led to another. I now live in Wimbledon, but my wife and I have a small house in Crete where we hope to spend an increasing amount of time in future.

I always enjoyed putting pen to paper, but never did any serious writing until a mid-life career change led me to the overseas property business via a company we started called Aegean Blue, which sells homes in Greece to UK and Irish buyers. A series of happy coincidences led to me writing about our house in Crete, and it has now become a very enjoyable sideline that makes a welcome occasional change to my day job of selling houses.

Greece is my specialist subject because of my family connections and of course the Aegean Blue business. But I would love to broaden my horizons and perhaps write a novel based in Greece; a friend of ours has done that very successfully. The notion of sitting at a small table overlooking the azure sea while tapping out a bestseller is very attractive!

The time I spend travelling each year varies, but it probably adds up to three to six months a year in Greece. In the early spring I travel around to different locations meeting developers and sellers, and I always try to be there when the buyers make their viewing trips.

I think I have forgotten how to write in longhand, so my laptop goes everywhere with me, as does a good digital SLR camera. My approach to photography is basically that the more photos I take, the greater the chance that I will take a good one, so I snap away and hope for the best. I usually seem to get lucky. I feel that the more personal a picture is, the more it complements my writing style.

I'm the sort of writer who gets a first draft down in next-to-no-time and then spends ages re-writing, fine-tuning, polishing-up and generally agonising over how to improve it. I often wonder if the finished product is actually any better than the original draft. Perhaps I should try just submitting my first attempt next time and see what reaction it gets!

These are my tips for people in the travel/property business who want to get into magazines:

► Personalise your style: there is no shortage of people writing for magazines, so you need to stand out from the crowd. A personal touch can make your column entertaining as well as informative.

► Have an angle which is clear to the reader from early in the piece so that they are hooked.

► Less is more – don't dwell on the detail unless it is essential.

► Double-check your facts: you may have a lot of knowledge and experience in a particular field, but that doesn't mean that one of your readers may not know more than you do!

► It's true – a picture is worth a thousand words, so always have a good range to choose from.

► When you are starting out, you need them more than they need you. Pursue relationships with editors on their terms and give them what they need rather than what you think they should want. Never compromise your principles, of course, but recognise that journalists have their priorities and usually work within constraints over which they have limited control.

► Read a lot before you start writing. Understand what already works for the publications you want to target, and identify the key elements need to incorporate into your own writing. There will be scope for letting your own style develop when you are established, but that is less important at the outset than becoming accepted.

► Having an area of expertise, a specialist subject, is very important. Getting under the skin of your subject is something that compels attention rather than the superficial approach which makes most readers want to move on to the next article.

► Don't become too emotionally attached to your writing; be prepared for the pain of rejection.

My favourite travel book is *The Colossus Of Maroussi* by Henry Miller. Published in 1941, it is a record of his impressions as he travelled across Greece. The combination of powerful writing, characters so real you can almost touch them and locations which I know and love is exceptional. Miller isn't my favourite writer, but this book captures the spirit of the country better than any other book I've read. **'**

8 – Market your travel articles

'Marketing is the art of making someone want something you have.'
~ The Internet Nonprofit Centre (1999)

This weekend, you'll have enjoyed the modules on writing – I know you have. How pleasant it would be, then, just to concentrate on the writing and never have to think about marketing your work, and yourself. It's not the most creative side of the business, but if you want to move your travel writing career on, if you want to get published, to see your work in print, it's unavoidable.

Marketing your work as a freelance writer isn't so different from marketing any other service. Writing can be certainly more enjoyable and fulfilling than many other occupations, but it's not so grand and important that it doesn't have to be marketed in a businesslike way.

I'm often surprised by the outdated and clumsy way some freelances try to market their work; methods they would scoff at if used by professional gardeners, plumbers or painters. An estate agent wouldn't send you marketing material, and then call you to ask you to return it. But I get what passes for marketing packages that include material – original photographs – which are clearly valuable and which the would-be writer obviously wants to have returned safely. It's crazy! When marketing your work, send nothing that has to be returned. Look at most newspapers and magazines, and somewhere in there you'll see a small paragraph in quite tiny print telling readers that the editors can take no responsibility for the loss of or damage to material sent to them. That little paragraph isn't there just to fill space!

There are other things that small businesses wanting your custom don't do. They don't:

▶ Ring you constantly demanding to know if you've read their publicity leaflet

▶ Quiz you on what you'd pay them, before you've even discussed the work you want done

▶ Send out flyers without contact information such as telephone numbers and e-mail and website addresses

▶ Speak rudely to you if you say thanks, but no thanks – they know that the nicer they aare, the more likely it is you'll use them in the future

▶ Comment on your house or your business "not looking very good, is it?", "you definitely need improvements" in the way some freelancers approach editors

If they have any commonsense at all, they certainly aren't rude to potential clients. A conversation I had with a former local newspaper editor shocked me – and I like to think I'm reasonably unshockable.

Responding to his inquiry about writing opportunities, I answered politely: "It's good of you to think of us. But I have to admit our rates are a little low – wouldn't they be too low for you?" I gave him an example, to which he replied: "I don't think your fees are low. I think they're crap." I'm all for plain-speaking, but this guy had taken a course in how not to influence people and win business.

If you politely tell a decorator, a caterer or a gardener that their estimate is too high for you, they would accept what you say and keep you on their mail-out list… just in case you change your mind or get a big lottery win. Freelance writers have to respond in the same way. An editor may have a low budget, but within a year the company set-up may have changed and he or she may have more cash to spend on freelance work. So keep them on your list of possibles, don't slam that door on them.

If you get a commission and agree the fee, don't fall into the Oliver Twist trap; don't ask for more. "May I have more for expenses… for petrol… for lunch… to pay for discs and stamps… for coffee and tea… parking fees… because I'll be making a lot of phone calls… because I'll be working over the weekend?" You need to make sure that these costs are factored into your agreed fee. That's what other professionals do.

7 marketing musts

▶ Be businesslike, not disorganized or too off-beat.

▶ Work out your minimum fee – and don't ask for more after it's been agreed.

▶ Invest in a little self-promotion. The more marketing packs you send out, the more you stand to gain. Widen your chances.

▶ Send editors a head-and-shoulders picture of yourself, for photo bylines. If you are successful, they'll want one, and they won't have to wait for it. Editors hate having to wait for pictures.

▶ Don't ask for cuttings and pictures to be returned; send copies.

▶ Don't play e-mail ping-pong, responding to a question from an editor with another question, or keep thinking up fresh things to quiz them about.

▶ Always carry business cards.

Write a press release – about you!

An important part of your marketing pack will be a press release about yourself, written in the third person. It isn't boasting, which I know is something we British don't take kindly to. It's a way of telling editors about yourself, and helping them to see how they could place your work.

Key phrases could be "dedicated backpacker", "Francophile", "travel writing award winner", "flamenco fan", "train travel expert", "advanced driver" – anything that indicates your areas of interest and expertise.

Here's how:

Judy Jones has spent 21 years travelling round Greece. She's lived in a cave in Crete, spent time in a monastery in Athens and worked in an art gallery on Rhodes. She speaks basic Greek and works as a freelance piano teacher when she's not writing about travel

Linda Mason asked for an unusual wedding gift – a cookery course in Italy. A keen dinner party hostess, she is a teacher of special needs children. Last year she won a short story competition for a women's magazine – she set her story in Florence.

Richard Jenkins began his travelling career as an airline steward back in the 70s, mostly doing routes to Palma and Glasgow. Now he's a civil servant in Bristol, but spends every holiday travelling in Europe, writing about it and building up his travel picture library. "I probably know Palma better than anyone in the West Country – but I now give Glasgow a miss!" he jokes.

Editors are always ready to welcome these sorts of writers.

And there's more . . .

When you make your opening pitch to editors, take the time and trouble to tell them about yourself. Don't just refer them to your website. I don't think I am alone in feeling annoyed that, when I ask writers for cuttings, I'm told: "Go to my website". Editors are under colossal pressure, with hundreds of details big and small to chase and supervise. So I want to see cuttings. I don't want to find a website – one that might not be working properly, might take a century to load and be difficult to navigate. I don't want to read features designed for magazine pages on a screen.

Move your marketing on

▶   If you meet an editor and you have an encouraging conversation, follow this up with an e-mail or letter instead of a telephone call.

▶   Buying small packs of envelopes and a half dozen stamps every so often isn't cost-effective; bite the bullet and buy them by the hundred if you can. Stationers such as Viking (www.viking-direct.co.uk) will often give ten per cent discount on bulk purchases, and orders worth £30 or more are delivered free. With stationery and stamps at the ready, you are more productive when marketing.

▶   Think in terms of doing larger "mail outs" – why not send your pack to 20 magazines instead of five? Get addresses from writers' yearbooks and *Writers' News* magazine.

▶   Get business cards printed; it's much cheaper to do this now. But make sure your card is readable, with clear typefaces and point sizes that won't strain the editor's eyes. Give all of your contact details – address, telephone numbers and e-mail address. Attach a card – or a compliments slip – to each mail out.

▶ Always have business cards with you, no matter where you are. I've handed them out in the supermarket, at a garage, at neighbourhood drinks parties.

▶ Try to reply to e-mails and telephone messages within 24 hours, and expect to pick up more work. The best way to do this – and not feel you're constantly on-line – is to timetable a half-hour at the same time every evening. Or, if it suits you, the first hour of your working day.

Recycle it!

Selling your work more than once is something that seems to make many freelance or hobby writers nervous. There's no need to be. It's your job to revamp with a new angle, thus increasing your revenue and your profile. What you may need to do is look further afield for your second and subsequent markets – they could be trade magazines, professional newsletters, women's magazines or newspapers.

How do you get those angles? There's only one way – by being curious. You need to ask questions. And then you need to ask follow-up questions. You need to get the detail.

For example, you're asking an interviewee which is their favourite holiday destination, and the short reply is "Italy" or "the USA".

That's not enough. Continue your probing with these sorts of questions:

Which part of Italy?

How many times have you visited?

Are you learning Italian?

What's your favourite Italian meal?

Why do you prefer the USA?

How many states have you visited?

What's the journey there you would most like to make?

What's the major difference between the UK and USA?

What USA trip do you suggest for the first-time visitor?

All you have to do is ask – and if you don't ask, you don't get.

Recycling shouldn't be an afterthought. Kick off with the intention of recycling it. Don't sell just a single feature on a topic. Check how many more magazines or newspapers might be interested – try the *Writers and Artists Yearbook* for this – or do some internet research.

Write your main feature for the market that pays best, then re-work it for the other possibilities. These will vary hugely. Often a travel feature for a mainstream publication can be expanded for different versions for trade and specialist magazines. This is an example of how I do it. The **first** feature – about hanging on to that holiday feeling when you're back at work, with lots of tips and suggestions – was for *The Guardian*. The **second** version was a piece about using a holiday week to take a course, with listings of courses that you could take and have a holiday simultaneously – time management on the Greek island of Skyros; learning French in Paris; a food and wine course in Florence; a creative writing course in Seattle. That was sold to *The Times* Crème features section. I sold a **third** adaptation to a Christian magazine, using the suggestions for women who wanted to holiday on their own and gain new skills. A **fourth** version, focusing on office skills you could gain from a holiday course, went to the *London Evening Standard*. I didn't run to a fifth!

7 easy tips for recycling travel features

CHANGE the introduction – make a third person intro into one that begins with a quote. Instead of "The new route to Lille is expected to attract thousands of people to this pretty French town", try "I'll admit it – I've never been that keen on France. Yet my weekend in Lille was one of my best holidays!"

CHANGE the ending.

ADD new quotes.

FIND a panel, box or sidebar which re-uses some of your original material in a new way – change opinions into tips and general advice into do's and don'ts.

START your piece earlier in the trip, or later – rather than your first meal there, begin with your last one. You instantly freshen up your story.

CHANGE adjectives to change the piece. If you've used adjectives such as sun-drenched… primitive… celebrated… remarkable, substitute scorching… basic… renowned… exemplary. Go through your piece inserting new adjectives for old.

DON'T use up all of your facts and quotes in one travel piece – save some for recycling. That way each separate piece has the vital "something different". A new picture also adds a new angle – take, or get, a selection of pictures of your subject if you can.

Plan ahead

Think about the various angles before you begin to re-jig your stories – even write down a running order. You can make a piece different by getting other views on the subject. For example, if you are writing about a new spa and leisure facility in your town, you could do one piece based on interviews with the people who work there, including their tips on fitness, and a second one about the people who are using the spa to get fit, with some background info about water therapies and perhaps a panel giving brief descriptions of some of the famous spas in Europe.

Pictures are a must

It's a cliché, but it's true: a good picture is worth a thousand words of your carefully sculpted prose. Photos are essential and, increasingly, as a free-lance writer, you'll be expected to supply them. The old industrial demarcation line between writers and photographers has been rubbed out, leaving only the mega-magazines such as *Hello!* with the mega-bucks to commission freelance photographers.

One of the first questions you'll be asked by editors of small- and medium-size magazines is: can you supply pictures as well as words? And, like it or not, you'll be paid little if anything for the pictures. They will be part of the package for which you'll get one quite modest payment.

If you are writing about your own city or region, you should be able to get fee-free images from the local authority's tourism or press office. Contact them when your feature has been accepted or when you've been given a commission.

Most magazines will accept large, high quality prints, while they're not so keen these days on handling transparencies, which have to be sent out-of-house to be scanned and then returned – all of which involves extra costs and the risk of damage or loss.

But the increasingly standard method of getting pictures to magazines is the jpeg computer format, filed by e-mail or sent on a disc, and most people now are using digital cameras to take their pictures.

If you are taking photos you intend to send to magazines – especially magazines printed on glossy paper – you'll need more than just any old digital camera. Magazines can use only high resolution images – a minimum of 300 dpi (that's *dots per inch*). If the resolution is lower than that, the picture's quality will deteriorate when it's used at the large size the editor may want – and which the picture may merit. You can make the picture look as big as you want on your computer screen, but that doesn't mean it's a high resolution shot.

To ensure you get those high resolution photographs, you'll need a digital camera with a minimum megapixel rating of six; anything less than this will give you photos good enough to produce decent prints or send to friends by e-mail, but they're unlikely to guarantee the quality and size needed for a glossy magazine. The higher the megapixels, the higher will be the picture quality you'll get – and, of course, the higher the camera's price tag.

Sorry, but pictures taken on mobile phones and from websites (even if you do own the copyright) will not be good enough.

Enhance sales

Here are some more ways in which to build up your sales:

▶ Make sure you send good-quality Christmas or New Year cards to editors who have bought work from you. My experience is that very few care much for e-cards. See if you can find real cards that relate in some way to writing or travel.

▶ When you send a completed commissioned piece to an editor, accompany it with a separate sheet of paper listing three new ideas you think would interest the journal for which you are writing.

▶ Anticipate requests for publicity photographs. If you are writing about a celebrity or local personality, they'll probably be able to give you pictures, which you can send in with your article; you will build up a reputation for being helpful and thinking ahead. But check first that the photos were not taken by a rival publication that owns the copyright.

▶ Add the extra "layers" the journal normally uses – for example, a fact file containing a booklist, buying details of products, travel contact information – anything that enhances the feature, helps the reader and fits in with the style of the publication.

My 8th Golden Rule

Invest in some marketing tools – business cards, pictures of you, a press pack. Never ask for anything back.

■ Case study: How Solange did it

Solange Hando, magazine travel writer and photographer.

Tell us about your early background, and where you live now?

I did an English degree at Nancy University in France. My first job was teaching French in a girls' grammar school in Ramsgate, which I did for more than 20 years. I live in Herne Bay, Kent, when I'm not travelling.

How did you get into the travel writing business?

A colleague suggested I write a piece for the school magazine after a family holiday in China. I loved the experience, which was an absolute revelation – this is what I was born to do! I enrolled on a correspondence course (David and Charles, forerunners of *Writers' News*) which taught me the most important lesson: marketing comes first. In 2000, I decided it was time for a change; well, it was the millennium! I gave up teaching to write full time and have never looked back. It's hard work but I love it; I could not imagine doing anything else.

Who published your first piece?

The school magazine, and that was followed by a double page spread in the local paper. After that, *Take a Break*, thanks to my 'wacky holiday pix', the sort of thing that was in demand at the time. No pun intended, but you could say that pictures gave me my first break – a point for any aspiring travel writer to bear in mind.

Do you specialise in any niche or any travel subject?

Travel is about places and people, so anything yields material, whether it's at home or abroad. I love the East, especially the Himalayas, and I visit France quite often – I was born there – but I do enjoy a change and a challenge, so I'll tackle anything. I do destination pieces, even though they're harder to sell; the odd interview or human interest story; quite a bit of history (I'm not a specialist, but I have a good market); and I do try to keep up with trends – week-end breaks, activity holidays such as painting, trekking, spa, or property related features.

How do you market yourself and your work, and get new commissions?

I post work and professional details on websites of the organisations I have joined (British Guild of Travel Writers, travelwritersUK, WPu, travelintelligence) and this has brought opportunities for syndication as well as commissions from new markets, sometimes quite unexpected. I'm currently involved with a *National Geographic* book; I didn't approach them, they approached me! I keep my regular markets well supplied with ideas, visit the newsagent to see what's new and follow up any leads. It doesn't matter how busy I am, I'm always looking for work, say 'yes' to anything, whatever the deadlines and then panic – but not for long – there's always a way to research or meet a deadline.

How much time every year do you spend travelling for your writing business?

On average, 12-15 trips a year, ranging from three days to three weeks.

Do you take a laptop or use a notebook – and do you take your own pictures?

A notebook, but no laptop – that's only an extra thing to carry and keep safe; looking after cameras is enough. I love taking pictures, and get far more excited when they are published than about the printed words, especially if it's a full page photo or a cover.

How important are production skills in handling photographs?

Mine are limited to basic image manipulation in Photoshop, and that's invaluable. It's also so much easier and cheaper to e-mail images rather than worry about slides.

How long does it take you to write your pieces?

Usually I have ten or more commissions ahead of me (fewer and I panic), so I have learned to work a lot faster than I used to. I'd say one to two-and-a-half days per piece, depending on length and the amount of research needed. Occasionally, I may have several pieces on the go if deadlines are tight, writing a first draft, polishing another, planning the next.

What's the secret of success in building up relationships with editors?

Joining professional organisations and attending travel shows and meetings. Whatever the topic, who knows who you might meet? Introduce yourself, leave your business card and once you've made contact, don't let it slip.

Who is your favourite writer?

I tend to read anything I find about the Himalayas – which I love – rather than choose a particular author.

Can you make a living just by your travel writing?

No chance of getting rich, but it's a brilliant life: travelling, writing, learning every day. No millions in the bank, but enough to survive as long as I find ways of financing the trips. If I can't secure a commission beforehand, and therefore a press trip, I'll consider hotel reviews and workshops, and talks on location.

Any pitfalls to watch out for?

Making promises you may not be able to keep, whether it's delivering work, or guaranteeing a commission or company credit, without checking with the editor first.

Any awards or prizes?

Writers' News Freelance Journalist of the Year, runner up in TNT and Thomas Cooke Archives travel writing competitions.

Are there any writing courses or magazines you would recommend?

Writers' News has stood me in good stead, but any course is only as good as your commitment and willingness to work hard.

What are your do's and don'ts for people starting out?

▶ Write for the readers, not yourself, and adapt content and style accordingly. See this as a challenge, not a betrayal of your own voice.

▶ Don't limit yourself to travel magazines; most publications have a travel page.

▶ Look out for a fresh angle; a well-focused piece is easier to sell and relevant interviews are always popular.

▶ Do as the editor asks, and check all your facts.

▶ Remember places on your doorstep; they may be home to you, but to someone else, it is travel.

▶ Travel writing is a highly competitive business; treat it as such. Before you do anything else, put your business plan down on paper. Be prepared to invest time, and probably money at first, before the press trips come rolling in.

9 – Be the favourite freelance

'Eighty per cent of success is showing up.'

~ Woody Allen

How much would your self-confidence be improved if you knew you were an editor's favourite freelance? Think that's impossible? Don't – I can give you all the soft skills to make you irresistible!

This is an important section, especially if you're feeling frustrated because you're not getting responses from editors, or because they seem to be taking their time in acknowledging your submissions. I'll give you some practical pointers, but this is an area in which emotions and the way you convey your personality can play a crucial part.

I have sabotaged at least two promising professional relationships in the past by answering the phone in a bad tempered way, and being dismissive of a feature editor's queries about my work. Yes, this was a long time ago – and I spent a long time regretting it! Now I make sure, when I'm in my freelance role, that no matter how simple, apparently trivial or inconvenient the query from a travel editor may be, my answer is always a polite yes. And when I'm in editor mode, I try to be helpful and generous (not in cash terms – that's beyond my control!) with my freelance contributors. They may – and probably do – say that I don't pay them enough, but I hope I can say that most of them don't dislike me.

The importance of being likeable and being liked is vital in freelance journalism. Being patient, tolerant, polite… they are all crucial virtues. Freelances can win or lose work by the way they deal with an editor. Anyone who talks to me on the phone or writes to me in a rude or arrogant way is unlikely to get work from me. Even if their writing skills are exemplary, there's no room in an over-stretched publishing office for carrying a trouble-making freelance. We haven't the time – and there are other, more flexible, writers waiting in the queue.

Learning the rules and the etiquette is much easier than you think. It isn't brain surgery or quantum physics. Most of it is common sense… and common courtesy.

The first thing to learn about being the favourite freelance is that what it doesn't involve is being pushy. When I started in journalism, the popular theory was that the harder you pushed, the more likely you were to succeed in the glamorous world of media. Not true. Yes, you need a degree of self-confidence – it's not the right profession for you if you are very shy – but strangers warm to you only if you are not overpowering. When we meet someone new, we're more likely to talk to him or her if they're non-threatening, not overbearing and have a pleasant voice and smile. Being modest and quiet opens doors for us, while being forceful and pushy can get them slammed in our face. The best description I've heard of the favourite freelance (from the editor of *The Lady*) was this: "Tried, tested and trusted", to which I would add "…and liked". Who wants to work with someone who's aggressive, touchy and arrogant? Yet sometimes, sadly, freelance writers display some or all of these qualities. This business is stressful enough without adding yet more pressure to it!

But there are plenty of "favourite freelances" to make up for the awkward characters. I have several favourites – they are all charming and easy to get along with. They're not demanding, and they're flexible. Yes, I tolerate two moody eccentrics, both of whom happen to be men! But they're basically well-mannered, and they're exceptionally good writers. But I couldn't manage any more of them. Travel journalism requires a pleasant and patient personality.

What does it all boil down to? Good manners – it's that simple. It's just a question of being polite, considering the needs of others, never demanding instant attention, and always trying to be helpful

Here are my three cardinal rules that will help you to be favourite freelance:

1: How not to be pushy

It's not being pushy that makes you popular with editors – it's being polite. Perfect manners will take you a long way – and keep you there.

When you ring, or want to talk about fees, speak to the editor as you might to someone you meet at a dinner party – with a slight reserve (you don't want to seem over familiar), moving to well-mannered friendliness. Good manners are vital, in e-mails, letters and phone calls. Be especially careful with e-mail – the "joking" remark from a freelance he or she doesn't know well does not look so good when it flips up in the editor's in-box.

Don't make comments about how wealthy the magazine must be, or how much revenue must be flowing in from advertising, or the huge sums you think the owners or shareholders must be taking from the business. Firstly, it's none of your business. Secondly, the company may be having trouble bringing in enough advertising revenue to make a profit.

Would you talk to your GP like this: "Why do you give me a miserable five minutes when you must be getting at least £80,000 a year?" Or even your hairdresser?: "Why do you keep me waiting 20 minutes when I give you £5 tips?" Build your relationships with editors politely; negotiate it through the ups and downs – and there will be some.

MAKE your first approach by letter, not e-mail or telephone. Attach your CV, a selection (no more than four) of any cuttings you may have, and three feature ideas for the magazine. If you don't hear back within a month, follow it with a polite e-mail. That rules out complaints such as, "Why haven't you been polite enough to answer my letter?" Editors are working with limited resources, their in-boxes are clogged up and time is usually running out on a deadline.

GIVE travel ideas to editors – don't ask for ideas to be given to you. We run out of them. We expect them from you!

ACCEPT criticism gracefully – and make the changes they ask for. Editors value your work, or they wouldn't bother to criticize; they'd just bin it.

DO NOT ask directly, or rudely, for more money. Of course you can raise the subject, but do it in writing, by e-mail or letter. Editors dislike free-lances who tell them, "Your money won't pay my son's school fees!" or, "I'm not going to get rich on what you pay me". I don't think I am responsible for someone else's school fees! Raise the topic politely: "As I have been writing for you for three years now, would you perhaps consider increasing the fee by £50?" Then outline some new ideas or benefits you could offer. Don't say you have been approached by rival magazines and offered more.

TAKE on the burden of doing all the work for each feature you write – don't expect the magazine's staff to do some of it for you. It may not have much of a staff! This includes fact boxes, airline and holiday company details, and – very important – a price for the holiday if it was taken by the reader.

DO not pitch new ideas before you have completed your current commissions.

DON'T ask when an editor wants features, or how much he or she can pay, before she has even commissioned them – take things at a steady pace.

BITE back any snappy comments, even if what the editor says is wrong or annoying. Once you've "had words" with an editor, it's hard to regain a congenial working relationship. You may be labelled as "difficult" and work from that magazine may dry up. Yes, some editors may well be the difficult ones. Tough! Humour them, put up with them, jolly them along. Don't make things worse.

2: Be businesslike

Yes, it's a creative industry – but you'll make friends and influence editors by being businesslike. That means pictures supplied as transparencies or prints being sent by Special Delivery, and with accurate, informative captions. If you're sending them on a disc or by e-mail, include a file with a list identifying each picture. It means invoices presented clearly and precisely. "Your invoices are a delight," I was once told by the editor of an international women's magazine. All I'd done was use lots of white space on crisp white copy paper, put all my details in a readable point size and clearly referenced the feature and fee. That's all! No fancy fonts, no titchy bits of tissue paper from lined invoice books, no unreadable handwriting. By contrast, I still occasionally get puzzling hand-written invoices scrawled on what looks like scrap paper – hardly an impressive advertisement for the writer!

EDITORS hate being told on the phone by someone to whom they have given a commission that the feature can't be done – three days from deadline! Always be reliable.

IF an editor asks for high resolution pictures – and they are what's needed for magazines – do not send low resolution versions. The picture content may be brilliant, but it's useless if at 300dpi it's the size of a postage stamp. If editors do not have usable pictures, they can't use your feature.

YOU are submitting feature copy, not wallpaper. Don't waste time with formats, boxes, colours and fancy bits and pieces added. A plain Word document is all we need.

THESE are words editors do not want to hear: "Oh, your editorial assistant/ sub-editor/picture editor/secretary should be able to deal with that bit of my work and finish it off." Surprise, surprise! I'm an editor and I don't have any of these servants. Neither does any editor I know. In many magazine offices, they're very 20th century. Please - submit work that's query-free and doesn't need any "finishing off". Don't leave any gaps for us to fill in.

NEVER quibble when asked to quickly re-vamp or change something. "Another 100 words you say? Well, I shall have to add £10 to the bill then. OK?"

My advice is – if the extra work is not significantly more time-consuming, then throw it in for goodwill. If it is, do it and add to the bill later on. Most editors in a hurry just want the work done. Do it fast and I'd be surprised if your slightly higher fee would be challenged. But, a warning: if you are asked to re-work something because your original effort was not up to standard, then forget asking for the extra tenner.

KEEP good records – keep a copy of all commissions, e-mails from editors, your own invoices and the fee advice notes sent from magazines. Not every magazine bothers with them – they may just send you a cheque, which can be baffling if you haven't kept a good record. Try numbering your invoices so you can check up on them.

3: Don't ring us – we'll ring you!

Yes, it still applies! Most editors dislike phone calls "on spec" at any time. We welcome calls from people we already know, but prefer on-spec queries in writing, accompanied by cuttings and a brief CV. Editors are always over-loaded with work, and you may call at an especially stressful time, on or near a deadline or in the middle of a crisis of some sort. By contrast, I love phone-in days when we invite readers to call us and chat. I'd do one every week if I could. The time is allotted just to that, so there's no conflict with other demands.

This doesn't mean you can't develop your relationship. As well as selling features, sell solutions. Look at the magazines that have bought your work, and ask yourself, "Is there something more I could offer them?" Maybe the magazine is crying out for a column you know you could do? If they have especially liked certain features you've written, could you suggest a series? Can you offer leads or links to new advertisers? There is never any harm in suggesting ways in which you can help the magazine grow. This strategy is often successful with start-ups, local magazines (which can often expand rapidly), and local newspapers. But don't ring – set out what you can offer, in bullet points, in a letter and, if you don't hear anything within a month or so, follow it up by e-mail. It's quite likely the editor will ring you!

IF you have a website, can you put the magazines you write for on it? Offer them a link? Think in terms of making partnerships with the editors you write for, rather than building up a "them and me" scenario.

TRY not to send anything which you want returned – send copies of pictures, or high resolution digitals. Then you'll never be ringing up asking for stuff to be sent back to you.

ALWAYS find a way of identifying pictures – if prints, a sticky label; if digitals, with a number that relates to a caption. Put each transparency in a separate envelope.

WHEN an editor rings you, make time for the call. Anything else – within reason, of course – can wait. Look on this as your marketing time, and you're not even paying for the call.

TRY to follow an editor's vocal style when they ring. If they're brisk and in a hurry, don't slow them down. If they want to chat – we do sometimes – chat.

Handle the editor with care

Most of the letters and queries I get on my *Writers News* helpline are about getting on – and how not to fall out – with editors; there seems to be no publishing arena where more offence is taken, more frustration expressed, more lack of understanding found, more difficulty experienced. But, once a contributor has been rude to or unreasonable with an editor, things will never be the same. No matter how good the writer's work, you just want to avoid dealing with them.

It's human nature – we all want to do business with people who are courteous and accommodating.

In this, the publishing business is much the same as any other. I'm often surprised by how effortlessly beginners and even successful freelances will sabotage their future prospects by a) taking needless offence at the way their work was used, or the timing of it b) trying to force an editor into a decision or c) simply pestering him or her for attention. Yes, I'll own up: I've made mistakes in this area, and I have tried to learn from them. It's so easy when you feel the editor is wrong, inexperienced or disorganised – or all three – to want to express your annoyance. But steel yourself: keep that criticism to yourself! Once someone has been even a little bit ubrupt or aggressive with us, we'll never feel the same about them! No matter how pleasant they are afterwards, we'll never forget the rudeness.

How not to do it

Just to show you how immature some would-be writers can be, here is a full and genuine account of an exchange between a travel writer – a beginner – and a travel editor. It will lift your spirits – since it's not something you would ever dream of doing!

The writer had turned in a very poor piece, which needed a huge amount of re-working by the more than somewhat busy editor. Names have been deleted to protect the foolish.

It kicks off with the contributor's e-mail:

Hi,

I was wondering when the issue of Cottage Holidays magazine featuring my trip to Wexford was out? If so, where can I pick up a copy, and whom should I invoice for payment?

Here's the editors reply:

Thanks for your note.

I hope you'll forgive me, firstly, for pointing out that the name of the magazine to which you've contributed is Holiday Cottages, not Cottage Holidays. I'm sure I sent a copy to you after your first approach to me. In any event, the magazine's name has been on some of the e-mails you've received from me.

Secondly, I regret that because your submitted copy required substantial editing work on my part - far more than I would expect to have to give to freelance features from professional writers - I am prepared to pay £100, not the £130 I offered when the piece was commissioned.

The feature will be in the issue that goes on sale on February 16. If you let me have an invoice for £100 (sent to me at the above address) I will mail a copy to you when we get them from the printer. Payment will be made by cheque by the end of the first week of March.

Regards,

To which the reply was:

Thanks for your kind note, and your generosity of spirit. I think it's great that people like you show encouragement and support to newer writers, especially those prepared to forego a week's wages and pay every single expense themselves to write a five-page feature AND take photos (which you described as 'good') for the handsome reward of £130.

Back then, when you approached me I was desperate for work. Newly redundant, and with a family to feed, I was taking everything offered to me. It was hard to believe that someone could offer £130 for a lengthy travel feature, as you did, but because I needed to work and establish myself, I took it.

I'm sorry you didn't like the piece, and that you sweated for weeks trying to turn it into readable English. You obviously think you deserve your £30, and I'm happy to give it you. In fact, I'm happy to give you the entire £130. Enjoy it. Do something nice with it. Brighten up your mean-spirited and petty-minded life a little. Go buy a good book, or smell some flowers. Take yourself out of your life for a while. It sounds like you need to.

Best wishes

This was the very patient but sorely-tested editor's reply:

I'm writing to acknowledge receipt of your e-mail in which you state you decline payment for your Wexford feature.

Regards,

And this was the by now ex-contributor's final word:

I couldn't give a rat's ass what you acknowledge. I wouldn't touch a penny from you lot.

Result – the editor's decision was final! Plus he let fellow editors know about this exchange, so the chances of fresh work for the ex-contributor were reduced – considerably.

E-mail info

Like it or not, e-mail is the industry standard for communications now. Use it properly.

Don't begin e-mails with Hi! or Good Morning, Diana! Or Hi You Guys! to editors you don't know or have never met. What's wrong with Dear Diana, or Dear Ms Cambridge?

There's no need to sign off "yours faithfully/sincerely". An e-mail is ideally a brisk, factual, polite and most of all speedy communication.

Format your e-mails – a space of two lines between each short paragraph is right. Don't ramble. Keep things crisp.

Don't use clichés such as "watch this space", "back to the grindstone" or "keep smiling". Just make your words say what you want them to say – the facts

Top tips

Promises, promises!

▶ Never take on a commission that includes pictures, and then tell the editor at the 11th hour that you can't deliver the pictures. It sometimes happens when interviewees in property or lifestyle-based travel features suddenly become camera shy and refuse to co-operate on the photo front. There's a simple solution here. All the writer has to do is to make it clear before they do the interview that pictures are essential. Ask for, and take the pictures first – then do the interview. You will be able to weed out time-wasters very easily – and avoid annoying your editor.

▶ Don't keep thinking of excuses for late work. We've heard them all before! The best thing is never to be late. To a travel journalist who sent me a piece three weeks late with the joky line, "Better late than never, eh?", I replied, "No, better never than late." I didn't use his work again. He was a freelance travel television presenter. Yet I have "ordinary" writers who are utterly reliable. They've never worked on TV, but I'd favour them every time over careless, arrogant and over-confident so-called professionals.

12 contact tips

1   On the phone, respond at the editor's pace. Match your tone and speed of voice to his or hers.

2   Never lose your temper on the phone, or sound as if you're angry.

3   Never send a rude e-mail.

4   Don't go above the editor's head to complain to the publisher about some imagined slight – you'll never get work from him or her again.

5   Deliver commissioned features before you suggest new ideas.

6   Always deliver copy and pictures on time – or, preferably and whenever possible, ahead of the deadline the editor has given to you.

7   Always supply pictures at the right size and format, with captions – send in on CD if possible.

8   Don't prolong conversations with busy travel editors. Don't worry if the conversation seems brisk – that's just a symptom of work! Show empathy.

9   Don't try to build up a relationship by asking time-wasting questions about the place where the magazine office happens to be – and how your aunt lives there.

10   Don't offer unnecessary information about your family life, or how busy you are, or how many other magazines – which of course are offering higher fees – are desperate for your work. Keep the conversation straightforward and professional.

11   Never launch into "How much do you pay?" before the editor has opened her mouth.

12   When on a press trip with other travel journalists, don't be tempted to bad-mouth or gossip about editors. Some of those colleagues could be the editor's friends – you could jump into a big hole. Comparing fees isn't a good idea either – be discreet.

Keep it going

Once you've started a relationship with an editor, you want to maintain it. Look after it, cultivate it, tend it carefully.

If an editor hasn't responded to your letter or e-mail, it's very probably because he or she is overwhelmed with work, and doesn't have a secretary or assistant. So don't keep sending e-mails that begin "Did you get my e-mail?" Be patient.

Suppose you've got on well with a certain editor, and had a few pieces published. Then a new editor comes on board. He or she is polite, but they don't take as much of your work. Soon the commissions dry up. What do you do?

First, don't send e-mails asking, "why don't you like my work?", or "what's wrong with my style?" Offer a few more ideas. If they are all turned down, don't focus on the problem. Sit it out. This editor may be moving on in a few months. Whatever you do, do not fall out with them. This has happened to me. I've been a magazine's favourite writer for several years, then a new editor arrives and suddenly I'm getting rejections. It just means the new person isn't in tune with your particular style, or else wants to call in people they already know; their own friends. Live with it – things will change.

In turn, when I've taken over at magazines, I have had to ease out the former editor's favoured writers – because I wasn't so keen on their style, and I preferred other writers for my version of the magazine. Every editor does it their way, and when newly appointed they want to make changes and aim for a "new look".

Practical checklist

PUT all of your contact details on every single communication you send, from a one-line e-mail to a feature. That's name, address, and phone number, e-mail address.

ONCE you have filed your article, try not to keep sending amendments and revisions – don't even send one unless it's essential. To avoid this, just do two things – read the copy twice at an hour's interval, checking all the facts. If you can leave it overnight, read it again the next day. Then send it.

UNDERSTAND that copy can get lost and e-mail boxes can get clogged up. When asked to re-send, do so quickly and don't say, "I have already sent it! What on earth happened to the first one?"

DO not try to impress by telling them about the exciting work you've been asked to do for other publications. They're interested only in what you do for them.

ALWAYS ring or e-mail them back promptly if they leave a message for you to do so – don't leave it until the next day.

WHEN taking a commission over the phone, do not ask them to e-mail you with all the details. Instead, write the details down and send them in an e-mail, asking for a one-line confirmation. Contributors who ask for every detail or guideline to be put in writing slow us down.

KEEP copy deadlines pinned up on your noticeboard, and if you have a regular column keep working well ahead. If you can get a whole issue ahead, you'll certainly be one of the editor's favourites.

TRY to avoid making too many requests of the editor – for example, for back issues and extra copies to send to friends.

NEVER dismiss a too-low fee rudely. For all you know, fees could be in the process of being raised – but once you're rude, they won't ask you again.

THINK of pictures you send – maybe of yourself – as non-returnable. Asking for pictures to be sent back just adds to the editor's workload and makes you look a little bit unprofessional.

SEND clear invoices very promptly, and don't put more than one piece of work on a single invoice. Accounts systems vary, but they much prefer, and some only recognise, single-item invoices, especially when different publication dates are involved.

DON'T think the editor can change the accounts system, especially for you. If they pay on publication, not on acceptance, it's something you have to accept.

Angry? Me?

How should you deal with your emotions if you feel annoyed or slighted by an editor?

Maybe all of your ideas have been rejected. Or you've put a piece in, only to be told "Can you change this? It doesn't read well". *Or*

"We'd like extra listings – the ones you've done aren't relevant". *Or*

"The intro's dull. Can you alter it?"

Rather than be tempted to snap back, pause for a moment and re-frame your thoughts. Think in terms of helping him or her. Keep that "how can I help?" thought in the front of your mind. It will automatically soften your voice as you make helpful suggestions – and you will find her voice softens as well.

Then there's the annoyance of filing a piece by an agreed deadline – perhaps meaning you work late or in a hurry – only to find that it's been held over for the next issue. You needn't have raced at all. Here's another blood pressure raiser – reading your piece in the magazine, but with someone else's byline on it! This has happened to me. It's annoying and frustrating, but I did not make a fuss – what's the point? I was cross, because I knew that it was an error that could have been spotted and amended. But it didn't make any difference to the reader, and I was still paid for the feature. Only my vanity was bruised.

When talking on the phone to an editor (or anyone) who has been the cause of irritation or anger, push your tongue to the top of your mouth – it instantly starts to relax and your voice won't sound tight. Try to smile, even though you aren't smiling inside – again, it smoothes your voice out. Inject a cheerful tone into your voice, even though it's an effort.

Remember, instead of feeling angry, replace that negative thought with "how can I help this person?" It does take effort and practice, but it does pay off. Try to weigh up the pleasure of letting rip against the pain of losing future work.

Top tip

Never forget that we can choose our behaviour! This has been drilled into me by my personal coach, Michael, over the years. I still have to work at it, though. But think about it – it gives you freedom.

My 9th Golden Rule

Be as polite to the travel editor as you'd be to your best friend – and always be reliable.

■ *Case study: How Gillian did it*

Gillian Thornton, freelance travel writer and photographer, specialising in French and UK travel, self-catering, city breaks and over-50s.

Starting out

I did A-levels in English, French and Italian, then a two-year bilingual secretarial/French civilisation course at the Institut Francais du Royaume-Uni in London. While in my first bilingual PA job in London, I started an evening class in Writing For Pleasure and Profit – two terms that eventually led to a whole new career.

I moved to a bilingual PA job at Kodak's European HQ in London, and in my spare time I wrote and sold features to county magazines, charity publications, etc. I joined Trusthouse Forte as PA to the public relations manager, all the time slowly breaking into women's magazines with general features. I married in 1980, and a year later I joined *Kodak News* – then a fortnightly staff newspaper - as a short-term freelance helping out during staff shortages. I took the plunge and went self-employed as a journalist. That's when I knew where my future lay. When I had my son, I carried on freelancing from home on company publications. My daughter was born in 1987. As my children grew, I simply re-invented myself according to family circumstances: I wrote for parenting titles as young mum, then back to general features and celeb interviews. I focused on travel from 1998. Living in Hertfordshire, I'm near Luton Airport, and fairly equidistant from Heathrow, Gatwick and Stansted.

The accidental traveller

I got into travel writing by accident. I'd written pieces about our family travels for a couple of women's magazines, but then two things happened by chance. The features editor of a magazine for which I'd written regular celebrity pieces and occasional travel articles was headhunted to launch an online travel magazine. He took me with him. Around this time, I was covering market research for *Writers' News*. While looking at the travel magazine sector, I got talking to the editor of a Francophile title, who asked me to look out for celebs with French connections. I found a couple. He offered me a press trip to do a destination feature. Within months, the balance of my work had shifted dramatically towards travel.

I sold my first travel piece to *My Weekly*; I have written more than 450 features for *My Weekly* over 18 years. Now I write regularly for *Living France, Destination France, Holiday Villas, Holiday Cottages, Active Life* and *My Weekly*, with sales also to *Yours, Take a Break, Greece, Italian magazine, The Travel Magazine*, and *The Traveller in France*.

Marketing me

How do I market myself and get commissions? I network at travel press events. I belong to organisations such as the British Guild of Travel Writers (I'm currently its secretary), Travelwriters UK, Writers and Photographers Unlimited, and Press4Travel. And I work hard at good relationships with like-minded editors.

I'm off – again

I probably set off on a trip every 10-14 days on average between early April and mid October; less frequently during the winter, as I don't do long haul or ski destinations. I do four or five complete weeks every year; other trips are usually three to four nights.

The writing bit

I take notes in shorthand in small spiralbound notebooks – they're great when you're on the move. If a deadline is pressing or I know there'll be time to write on a plane or train, I take a laptop. Otherwise, I don't start writing until the trip is finished and I know exactly how I'm going to approach the piece. I always take my own high resolution digital images. I can produce a clean manuscript – well laid out and correctly spelt – and I can provide high quality images on disc. My production skills stop there, and so far it's never been a problem.

Once I've written the opening – the hardest bit of all – I'm away. I can do a 2,000-word piece comfortably in a day, but would always want to polish it after a good night's sleep. One magazine buys a 4,000-word in-depth feature, which takes more than twice the time of a 2,000 piece; the crafting is harder and there are more facts to check. I'd allow two-and-a-half to three days for that. But there are days when turning on the creativity is like stirring cold glue – we all get them for all kinds of reasons. When that happens, the best thing to do is walk away for a few hours and do something completely different.

Handling editors

Always do what you say you'll do, when you say you'll do it – if not before! Be reliable, consistent and nice to deal with. Simple, really!

Favourite writer

Bill Bryson, because he opens my eyes to new places and makes me laugh. That's a winning combination.

Pitfalls

Rates go down, not up. For every door that opens, two close. It's a highly competitive industry in which making a living is getting harder every year. Good thing we all love it!

Awards

Runner up, Best French Article 2005, Association of British Travel Organisers to France – a piece about Burgundy's new blackcurrant trail; also shortlisted for a second piece on Corsica.

Recommended

Writers' News/Writing magazine for general advice on writing; The British Guild of Travel Writers for people who earn a significant amount of their income from travel; International Travel Writers Alliance for its monthly e-mail newsletter.

Do's and don'ts

Don't think you're going to swan round the world for free, writing a little as you go – it's a tough industry to break into, and it's even tougher staying there. But if you have a burning desire to see the world – far away or on your doorstep – and to share your experiences with others, then have a go. You never know until you try.

10 – Keep travelling

'Travel gives me the opportunity to walk through the sectors of cities where one can clearly see the passage of time.'

~ Jerzy Kosinski

We're at the last stage of the weekend course. You've stayed with it. I've been at your side for 48 hours. And you've done brilliantly! You've studied, you've made notes, you've thought about what you're going to write and you should have your first piece written and in the envelope ready for posting. This in itself is a triumph – but I want you to keep travelling and above all keep writing.

Think about entering travel writing competitions – and competitions that aren't for travel writing. With a little re-angling, you may be able to turn your piece about your 48-hour second honeymoon in Berlin into a relationship piece for a women's magazine, or even a short story. The feature about a French cookery course in Lille, travelling by Eurostar, might be snapped up by a food magazine, or the "courses" section of a magazine or newspaper.

Be a winner!

Always write a travel piece with the intention of entering it later on for a writing competition. What have you got to lose? File a paper copy, and a copy on your computer, and when you see an advertisement for a travel writing contest, you've got something ready. It might need just a little updating.

I organise the judging of the annual travel writing competition for *Greece*, the monthly glossy magazine I edit. While the overall standard is high, some of the entries, about a third, eliminate themselves on the first sifting. They fail because they:

Cover too much in 1,200 words

Are boring, plodding descriptions of a holiday

Were lists of the good points only

Began at the luggage carousel

Read like a travel company brochure

Lacked any sort of 'story'

Used clichés for description

A possible winner can be spotted within the first few sentences. The feature engages you instantly because there's something there that tells you it will be different and honest, and that it will give the reader benefits. Here are a few examples. They're similar to winning articles I have picked in my travel writing competitions.

> *I was jolted from sleep at 3a.m. by the deafening sounds of rock'n'roll. Early Rolling Stones! The disco on the other side of the olive grove in Santorini had just begun.*

> *"So what exactly is diet food here?" My companion looked doubt-fully at the lavish, calorific menu on our holiday in Rome.*

> *"No, there are no 'facilities' on this walk". The German walking guide was stern. So – a six hour trek through the castle-dotted countryside, but without bathrooms…*

Here's what I chose in another writing competition I judged. You'll see that the original idea is the one most likely to succeed.

The first prize was won by a woman writing about her birthday gift, a "mystery" holiday that turned out to be a yoga vacation in Spain. The runner-up was a feature about a couple taking a weekend trip to Iceland for their 25th wedding anniversary, while the third prize went to another couple and the writer's account about their "foodie" trip to France.

The winners packed their pieces with plenty of facts, anecdotes and personal views – stimulating and entertaining reading. Travel could be a trip to Frome or Florida, Portishead or Prague or St. Petersburg. All that matters is that your words bounce off the page.

Editor's tips

The former *Northern Echo* editor and current editor of both *Holiday Villas* and *Holiday Cottages* travel magazines, David Kernek, says that when reading features sent to him by contributors, and judging travel writing contests, he has this very clear idea what he wants:

"I look, at the very least, for a piece that's informative and accurate. It has to be written grammatically so that I can understand the information, and I want it to convey something about the atmosphere and flavour of the destination. If I'm entertained by the writer's humour and get a sense of his or her personality, then that's a bonus."

His tips are:

▶ Write for your readers, who are looking for different places to visit. Look for different things to tell them about, if only briefly. Keep your eyes open for the unusual. Your job is to notice things other people miss.

▶ Be disciplined. You're providing an informative and practical overview, not a street-by-street guidebook or a detailed history. Organise your material, in separate sections if necessary, and write tightly.

▶ Use humour and irony. Humour is at a premium; editors welcome it, provided their sense of humour matches yours! When a judge is sifting 200-plus entries, something that makes him or her smile could be on the way to the first shortlist.

▶ I find inconsistency maddening – for example, don't give some distances in miles and then swing into kilometres for others. The same goes for prices. Avoid exotic cocktails of £s, $s and €s. Choose one (preferably the £), and stick with it.

How not to give up

Here are some ideas for getting going during a dry patch:

IF magazines have phone-in days for readers, phone in! You get to speak to the editor (I talk to everyone who calls on my phone-in days) when you can mention a topic he or she may take up later.

READ newspapers and magazines for travel news. New route to Krakow from your local airport? The start of a £40 weekly flight to Naples? Cheap flight for a ski trip to Poland? These are ideas you could mine.

WORK on a piece you could enter for a competition… even if you haven't yet seen one advertised. Make notes, draft intros – when a competition presents itself, all you'll need to do, perhaps, is re-slant it, cut it or add material to fit in with the rules. That's much better than having to create something completely new for a competition when the cupboard is bare.

AS you're working, play music that inspires you. For me, that might be anything from Bob Dylan's *Modern Times* to Tom Waits or The Rolling Stones to fugues by J.S. Bach. Listen to something that's invigorating.

KEEP a bottle of mineral water on your desk. I can't count the number of times I've flagged, then felt revived just by swigging glasses of water. It really does re-energise your system.

TAKE a short, achievable course that will enhance your travel writing. It could be digital photography, wine appreciation or a sampler course in a foreign language. And you needn't sign up for months of classes; day or weekend courses can be very inspiring.

Cope with criticism!

Rejection could be more likely in travel writing than in any other branch of the business, but if your work interests an editor, it's also the most likely genre to have slots for regulars. Reliable writers with pleasant personalities, who can provide good pictures and don't mind re-vamping or adding material, are like gold dust.

Every editor I know wants to build up a team of these paragons. My team is composed of exceptional writers, all of whom started out in different jobs, not as journalists. Some of them still have their day jobs; they're amateurs, in the very best sense of the word – they love what they do, and they do it well.

We don't pay much – few travel magazines do – but I try to give them profile where I can. I like to use their pictures on the Welcome Page, with little details about them each time. I'll do all I can, as far as I can, to help their writing careers. There's always room for the gifted newcomer, and it's essential for magazines to regularly introduce new faces.

There may be a problem or two when someone new comes in – their style may need adjusting, or they haven't polished their feature well enough. I may have to criticise their work. Some writers are downcast by this – they give up and I hear no more from them. But most ride out early hiccups, stay positive, keep the magazine's needs in mind and become our regulars. Editors welcome the talented novice who is also easy to deal with, accepts criticisms gracefully and copes with his or her idea being turned down once in a while.

Follow it up

You have had a travel piece published, maybe in *The Lady, The Guardian,* or *The Observer* (these are all good freelance hosts). Your next step must be to:

▶ Follow up with three more ideas to the same editor.

▶ Approach other publications with ideas.

▶ Plan your next holiday with writing it in mind.

▶ Think about creating a travel piece from a UK break.

▶ Get 20 photocopies of the published feature to send out as part of your marketing pitch – it's much easier to commission from a writer who has sent cuttings.

▶ Take travel courses and workshops – you will find them listed in *Writers' News* magazine, and at literary festivals and local authority adult education offices. Keep the notes and start building up your own travel writing archive.

You're a travel writer now!

Finally, here are my ten practical steps to travel writing. Refer to them – as well as my Ten Golden Rules – whenever you feel tired, jaded, depressed or lacking in confidence. And you can always e-mail me at my writing club, diana@canalstreet.org.uk – I reply to every email!

Step One – Begin with the end in mind

If you're back from your holiday and thinking, "Who can I send my article to?" it's already too late! Decide before you go who you'll market to and why – if you have the opportunity and flexibility, plan your trip around the piece you're going to write. Your travel opportunity could be:

A week's holiday

Weekend break

A day trip

A holiday learning or activity course

Going somewhere new for your work

A trip to visit a "sight" – perhaps The London Eye or the Houses of Parliament

"24 hours in Paris... ", or even "8 hours in Dublin..." – use different formats

A cold weather break, such as a short winter holiday in Iceland, Lapland or Norway

The publication you'll be aiming at should be one you know quite well and preferably read regularly. It could be *The Lady, The Independent*, a cycling journal, a women's magazine or *Saga* – but you must know its style and readership. Even looking at the ads will tell you something about the reader – are coach holidays and stairlifts advertised, or cut-price flights and Palm Pilots.

Hot tip: Think in terms of helping your reader.

Ignore the expensive restaurant at Bristol airport. There's a very good capuccino bar with delicious cakes near the entrance.

Step Two – Facts are on expenses

Comment is free, but facts are on expenses, to quote Tom Stoppard.

Your feature needs to be an alchemy of facts and colour, but do not cram the piece with so much information about prices, distances, opening times and history that it reads like a text book. I'd say a third facts and two thirds colour is about right.

Keep a diary as you travel – your reporter's notebook. Don't rely on your memory.

Note down facts – even price of cup of coffee

Talk to local people and other travellers

See alternative sights as well as the obvious ones

Collect photographs, postcards etc

Notice your first impressions airport, taxis etc, as well as your final impressions.

Hot tip: Don't try to write the feature while you're there; just take notes. And remember that adventures and mishaps help your piece. A bad time, too, is worth reading about – maybe more so!

Step Three – Layer it on

To make your travel pieces interesting and commercial, you need your main chunk of copy PLUS extras that give readers practical info and help editors to make the feature look attractive. These could be:

Tips – bring these (herbal pills) – don't bring this (travel iron)

Plus and minus points

3 quietest beaches

4 best cafes

5 things not to eat

Always include a factfile: how to get there, how to get around when you do get there, best time to go weather-wise, accommodation options and useful telephone numbers and websites for readers who want more information.

Hot tip: A touch of humour is very useful.

Step Four – Be stylish!

Dig out quotes from famous people about your holiday destination. You can also use comments from travel companions or from waiters, hotel staff, couriers – and they don't have to be flattering. They can be ironic or ambiguous, too.

Add style by using food – dishes, menus, and even short recipes that convey the flavour of the place.

Hot tip: You'll find lots of information and research for your article at any of the new bookshops that have sprung up specialising in travel: also use country websites.

Step Five – Present with polish

The more complete and groomed your work, the better. Magazines and newspapers run on very lean teams (some would say skeletal) so your features must slot in without needing masses of extra work. Your copy should be as taut as fiction but as informative as a news bulletin. Don't expect there to be someone at the office who will "go through" it to fill in the gaps, correct your spelling, amend mistakes and clarify ambiguities. The odd error will be corrected, but if your feature is sprinkled with them, it's likely to be spiked. Correct spelling of foreign names, places and foods – and correct facts about the country – are vital.

If you can e-mail your work, so much the better, but send a hard copy as well. Otherwise, send a disc, plus the hard copy double-spaced. And the all-important pictures, including one of you.

Hot tip: Pull-out quotes – one or two telling sentences from your text – give the editor a quick pathway to the story, and they've also become common, almost compulsory, newspaper and magazine design devices that help to draw the reader into the feature. Here are some examples:

> *'I slowly realised there wasn't another boat for two days'*

> *'New York has the best and biggest bookshops on the east coast – bliss'*

> *'Hay on Wye has a circus quality… expect to meet some eccentrics'*

Go through your piece and literally pull out the quotes which seem to sum it up. List them at the start of the main text.

Step Six – Do your own PR

You need to include a paragraph about yourself when you send off your piece. If you've published a book or edited a parish magazine – put that in. Customise your potted public relations biographies according to the magazine you're aiming at – for a cycling publication, mention your daily bike ride; for a food magazine, it's your interest in organic recipes.

Include all of your contact details – phone and fax numbers, and e-mail addresses, plus two or three cuttings if you've already had something published.

Get at least 20 copies of that good photo of yourself ready to send out. They can be done very cheaply, in WH Smith, Boots or at photo shops.

Have headed notepaper and business cards – maybe illustrated with something eye-catching, such as a travel bag, a cycle, or a boat. Clever computer people should be able to create something good – or pay a teenager to do it for you!

Hot tip: Always send copies of photographs and valuable documents, never originals.

Step Seven – Stay on the move

This doesn't mean you have to be constantly travelling. What it does mean is that you should always have several projects on the go. They could be a couple of travel articles, perhaps, a reader's letter about travel, notes for a short story set in a holiday destination. When you have something accepted it's a great achievement – don't let this pass. Celebrate it! Send them more travel ideas straight away – don't forget they need short and long pieces, so even a snippet may do.

Your dry spell is now? You can start this exercise in the next hour and finish it in a weekend. Try an 800-word piece on your town or city, written as if you were a visitor. Decide which magazine or newspaper you'd like to see it in, and follow its general style. Include the factfile and the pull-out quotes, as well as tips and do's and don'ts. Print it. Put it a stamped envelope. Send it out!

Hot tip: When you get a feature accepted, send the editor more travel ideas straight away – don't forget they need short and long pieces, so even a snippet may do.

Step Eight – Be curious

See life as a question mark. As you move around, think about the way people live and work in different places. Is the way of life very different in England's north-east to the way it is in Bath or Oxford? Is there a difference in the tourist attractions of say, Cardiff, to those in Cheltenham? What are the differences in regional food tastes and specialities? How does each place you visit affect you emotionally?

Hot tip: Go to a place – church, castle, bridge – in your new destination and just stand there for a while picking up the vibes. See what mood it places you in. Make notes.

Step Nine – Don't despair

Yes, you will face rejection from time to time. It may not mean a thing. It could just be that yours was the right article submitted at the wrong time for the magazine. That's all! It's essential not to give in to depression – you are not at fault.

Hot tip: Ignore rejection completely. Send out a new piece – or the same piece re-angled – the same day.

Step Ten – Record the journey

Record every journey! This applies to life, as well as just the business of travel. Keep observing, keep noticing, and never lose your curiosity. Life is composed of nothing but journeys. You, the writer, can enhance your own life just by writing it all down. Try it for a month, making notes in your personal notebook every evening, and see how much more positive and vital you feel. I'll guarantee it!

Hot tip: Adopt the discipline of writing every single day. Even a few words, a few phrases, are enough.

My 10th Golden Rule

Write every one of your travel articles as though it's for a travel writing competition.

■ Case study: How Rob did it

Rob Adams, music/travel writer for *Greece* magazine.

I was born in Liverpool and educated at a traditional grammar school for boys, where the teachers (masters, as we had to call them) still wore flowing black gowns and were not averse to commenting on bad behaviour by way of an old slipper or plimsoll.

I always wanted to be an archaeologist, but a misunderstanding over the importance of Latin steered me towards art college instead. It did, however, provide me with a good grounding in western classical music. After school, I completed a one-year foundation course in art and design, in an atmosphere still strong with the not-too-distantly departed John Lennon and other Liverpool luminaries of the late 60s and early 70s. I moved to Coventry to do a three-year fine art degree course, but fell foul of lack of money and my naivety, and left after 18 months. To cut a long story short, I eventually found myself working with adults with learning disabilities, a job I've been doing for 17 years, and find endlessly fascinating and fulfilling.

I have always had a huge interest in history, particularly the Bronze Age in Asia Minor, and the Trojan War. This, in my mind, comes together with an enquiring interest in music, ending in a love of Greek and Middle Eastern culture. I find most western music formulaic and in thrall to American tastes, so it was a natural journey that led me to discover Greek music, which is not ashamed of its eastern influences. My particular favourites are rebetika and traditional Cretan music, but there is a wealth of invention in Greek music as a whole, which often makes me feel like a child in a massive toyshop.

How did I get into travel writing? I was flying home from Athens in 2004 and decided after my second drink to write to *Greece* magazine, which I felt lacked coverage of an integral aspect of Greek culture – music. I had never done this sort of thing before, but I realised the time was right for me personally, and I would always regret it if I didn't. For quite a few years I'd been keeping travel journals with comments, thoughts and caricatures of people I'd met and situations I had observed. Of probably dubious quality, they nevertheless gave me the confidence to give it a go.

All my published writing has been about Greek music and dance, but I have a wide range of interests and, time allowing, I'd like to reflect these more. I am willing to give anything a go; I think it is important to stretch oneself.

I always write on holiday, and try to spend time at home mulling over thoughts, experiences and ideas. When I am away, I use notebooks and take photographs. At home, I write straight onto the desktop computer, usually serenaded by music, which helps my concentration and imaginative processes. I think a laptop might be on my Christmas list next year; I find writing in notebooks very time consuming, and I'm always afraid of missing the very experiences I may want to write about. I spend a lot of time just thinking. I was recently described as being a ruminative person, and that's probably an accurate observation.

The time it takes to write a piece can vary. Because it is not a full-time activity, I tend to spend around two hours a day, spread over three days. Each piece goes through a drafting process in which I leave it alone for a few hours and go back to it with eyes and mind refreshed. It's an approach that worked for me when producing paintings and drawings, where I would turn a canvas to the wall and put it out of my mind. When you return to the piece, you have a renewed clarity of mind and vision.

My advice to writers is that they should be themselves; don't try to be something they're not. Try to write in a relaxed state of mind, and never be disheartened. If you have someone who you can trust to give a truly honest opinion of your writing, use them and absorb what they say. They may not be right, but I think it is always worth consideration.

It's also important to find an angle; some little thing around which to weave your subject. It can add that extra element of interest for the reader to latch on to.

I should also say that writers should try not to be too long-winded. I've failed in writing this, but I hope some of it will be useful.

Diana's Ten Golden Rules
for writing travel articles in one weekend

1   Buy your first travel notebook now. Keep it with you at all times.

2   Decide what you'll do for your travel article and where you'll go.
     Jot down three angles on it now.

3   Do a free local travel journey next week – with your notebook in hand.

4   Plan a Gap holiday you could write about. Send for the details, or
     print them from the website, now.

5   All your travel pieces must have a beginning, middle and end –
     and a factbox.

6   Sell travel articles on food by writing about budget eats, or writing about
     cookery holidays.

7   You will succeed in travel/property writing if you follow the editor's
     agenda, not your own. Great benefits will follow.

8   Invest in some marketing tools – business cards, pictures of you,
     a press pack. Never ask for anything back.

9   Be as polite to the travel editor as you'd be to your best friend – and
     always be reliable.

10   Write every one of your travel articles as though it's for a travel writing
     competition.

Travel Writing Directory

Here are possible outlets for your work – and some extra resources for inspiration.

Australia & New Zealand magazine

£3.75, available from all good newsagents, published by Merricks Media, 01225 786800, www.merricksmedia.co.uk

Perhaps you've lived, worked or travelled Down Under or maybe you're planning a trip there – either way, why not pitch your travel ideas to the only monthly UK magazine dedicated to Australia and New Zealand.

Florida and the Caribbean magazine

£3.75, available from all good newsagents, published by Merricks Media, 01225 786800, www.merricksmedia.co.uk

Again, this is the only UK monthly magazine available on the market which is entirely devoted to Florida and the Caribbean. So if you have a great travel story which would be relevant to this magazine – then why not share it?

French magazine

£3.99, available from all good newsagents, published by Merricks Media, 01225 786800, www.merricksmedia.co.uk

As one of the leading travel titles for people who love France, this is the perfect magazine to submit your work to – especially if you are an expert of France – whether that be on French cuisine, culture, the property market or just on the best places to visit.

Greece magazine

£3.75, available from all good newsagents, published by Merricks Media, 01225 786800, www.merricksmedia.co.uk

Created entirely for people who love all things Greek – this club-style magazine consists of features on food, wine, property and travel and even holds its own annual travel writing competition. Previous winners have ended up becoming regular freelancers on the magazine too.

The Italian magazine

£3.75, available from all good newsagents, published by Merricks Media, 01225 786800, www.merricksmedia.co.uk

Another travel title produced by Merricks Media, the UK's no. 1 travel and property publishers. This classy magazine offers an inspirational and informative mix of features solely on Italy.

Spanish magazine

£3.75, available from all good newsagents, published by Merricks Media, 01225 786800, www.merricksmedia.co.uk

Covering every aspect of Spain from the burgeoning property market, to city guides, food and wine, to articles on Spanish culture and lifestyle, this really could be the ideal magazine for submitting your Spanish travel articles to.

Portugal magazine

£3.75, available from all good newsagents, published by Merricks Media,
01225 786800, www.merricksmedia.co.uk

Is your travel piece about Portugal? This glossy magazine provides information on Portuguese history and culture, hidden places to discover.

easyJet Inflight magazine

Available onboard most of easyJet's flights, www.easyjetinflight.com,

If you want your work to be read by millions of readers – then easyJet Inflight Magazine could be the ideal publication for you. With features on travel, property and business each month as well as reviews and much more – getting your work published in an in-flight magazine would make a great kick-start to your travel journalism career.

Wanderlust

£3.80, available in all good newsagents, Wanderlust Publications Limited,
01753 620426, www.wanderlust.co.uk

Featuring brilliant inspirational travel writing, this magazine is a key player in the field of travel publishing. And it's not just for readers who love to travel, but more for those who are particularly committed to special-interest travel.

Condé Nast Traveller

£3.60, available in all good newsagents, Condé Nast Publications UK ltd,
www.condenast.co.uk

The crème de la crème of travel magazines – Condé Nast Traveller is packed with stunning photography, great features and is incredibly informative and uncovers the best unknown destinations too.

The Sunday Times Travel magazine

£3.25, available in all good newsagents, River Publishing,
020 7306 0304, www.therivergroup.co.uk

If you are a fan of the Sunday Times travel supplement, then you'll love this glossy monthly magazine which is jam packed with inspirational ideas for exciting vacations. Failing that, it makes a great read, even for the armchair traveller!

A Place in the Sun magazine

£3.50, available in all good newsagents, Brooklands Group,
www.aplaceinthesunmag.co.uk

Aimed at those who want to move or buy a second home overseas, this magazine enables you to focus your travel piece on the property market – and with so many people now buying a home overseas – there's a lot of mileage in writing these sort of property articles.

Writers' Forum

£3.50, available in all good newsagents, 01202 589828, www.writers-forum.com

Get inspired by this popular writing magazine which is dedicated to writers of all genres. There are also opportunities to see your work in print as well as useful articles on travel writing itself.

Writers' Journal

£4.95. available in Borders and on subscription, www.writersjournal.com

This American magazine provides great articles and tips on writing in general, plus you can even enter their annual travel writing competition.

Spa World magazine

£3.00, subscription and distributed to salons etc, 01943 851 400, www.spaworld.tv

Travel writing needn't just focus on a country or undiscovered place – it can involve activities too, like for example, spas – an area which is experiencing rapid growth, especially within the tourism industry. This colourful magazine contains features and reviews of spas in both the UK and overseas – so it's worth considering.

Adventure Travel magazine

available in all good newsagents and specialist retailers,
01789 450000, www.atmagazine.co.uk

Specialising in outdoor activities throughout the world, this magazine is designed for those who love nothing more than fresh air and adventures. So if you're a bit of a thrill-seeker yourself, then perhaps some of your adventurous travel tales could be published here.

Luxury Spa Finder magazine

£4.00, available in all good newsagents, www.spafinder.com

This lovely magazine concentrates on the most luxurious spas and all things lifestyle –related. Another great place to try and publish your work.

Food and Travel magazine

£3.50, available in all good newsagents, 020 7501 0511, www.foodandtravel.com

The combination of food and travel sounds like heaven to some people and this delightful magazine features a heady mixture of both. So if you're an expert on foreign cuisine and travel or you have the perfect idea up your sleeve for unknown destinations and exotic food, then this is also a great magazine for pitching your ideas to.

Coast magazine

£2.99, available in all good newsagents, The National Magazine Company,
020 7439 5000, www.coastmagazine.co.uk

Celebrating everything to do with living by the sea, this stunning magazine includes a travel section with features ranging from hotel reviews to weekend getaways by the coast. A good magazine to get your work published in.

Real Travel magazine

£2.99, available in all good newsagents, Create Publishing,
0117 945 1913, www.realtravelmag.com

Boasting inspiring travel features on new destinations, plus advice and tips from readers and expert travellers. This informative magazine is more about the real traveller and includes reviews of the best travelling kit.

Holiday Villas and Holiday Cottages

www.villaspeak.com and www.holidaycottages.cc

These are big glossies, both published seven times a year. Holiday Cottages covers the UK and ireland, while Holiday Villas covers the rest of the world, majoring on the USA, the Caribbean, the Med plus emerging tourist markets such as Eastern Europe. Both magazines look for resort and country features – but don't forget both are aimed at people who want to rent houses and apartments for self-catering holidays. Both on sale in major supermarkets and newsagents. There's plenty of possibilities here if you angle your work carefully!

Useful websites:

Travel Writing Tips

www.travelwritingtips.com

Get tips on how to become a professional travel writer as well as how to improve your own work.

The Travel Writing Portal

www.transitionsabroad.com

Promising to be an honest account on the art of travel writing – there's plenty of advice and info to get you started or to help you improve.

Travel Insights

www.travelinsights.org

Join this online travel community – which it boasts - is a place to get inspired.

Travel Writers

www.travelwriters.com

A place where writers, editors, tour operators and PR agencies can meet and is an extremely valuable tool.

Writing.org

www.writing.org

Despite being American-based, the writer of this website has provided some very useful hints and tips for breaking into the travel writing market.

The Insider Secrets of Freelance Travel Writing

www.freelancetravelwriter.com

Aimed at teaching you how to become a successful travel writer – you'll find free articles on this website, which are both inspirational and informative. Plus there is also an online article critique service available too.

JournoBiz.com

www.journobiz.com

A great journalist resource, including many member benefits, along with the latest news, reviews plus events and training.

National Union of Journalists

www.nuj.org.uk

The union for journalists in Britain and Ireland – which boasts a website brimming with information specifically for aspiring and working journalists.

The Writers' Bureau

www.writersbureau.com

The Writers' Bureau offers useful home-study courses with your own private tutor, such as the Article Writing Course or the Freelance Journalism Course.

British Guild of Travel Writers

www.bgtw.org

This important organisation will tell you exactly who is who in the travel industry. Plus as a member you will receive many benefits, including a monthly magazine, discounts, plus much more.

Chartered Institute of Journalists Travel Writers

www.cioj.co.uk

As the oldest professional body for journalists, which campaigns for improved working conditions for journalists and much more, this website is essential for those looking to become a full time journalist who wish to protect their rights.

Travelwriters UK

www.travelwriters.co.uk

An excellent resource for travel writers, which allows you to create your own web page on the site and also has links to help you with your research.

Women in Journalism

www.womeninjournalism.co.uk

This organisation was created to help represent women working in senior roles in the media. It is a now a really useful forum for women journalists with plenty to keep you informed plus there are also opportunities for networking.

The International Travel Writers Alliance

www.internationaltravelwritersalliance.com

Providing essential information for travel writers, this well-renowned Alliance requires no joining fee or lengthy application procedure. There are over 3,600 travel writers currently part of the Alliance.

Travel writing and Travel photography courses

Travellers' Tales

Various dates offered throughout the year, www.travellerstales.org

Offering exiting courses in travel writing and travel photography, in a whole host of locations from Marrakech to Tuscany and Paris; Travellers' Tales combine sightseeing with expert tuition. Teachers include the editor in chief of Wanderlust magazine and author of the popular travel book 'Driving Over Lemons.'

Creative Writing Course: Find your Writer's Voice

Farncombe Estate, May 16-18 2008, 01386 854100, www.farncombeestate.com

Overcome the self-critic within you and learn how to write using your own unique voice in this motivating and inspiring course located in the beautiful Cotswolds.

Luxury weekend and week courses in the UK and overseas:

Travel Writing and various creative writing courses

Planned from February to November 2008 in Andalucía, Spain, from £679 including flights, half-board accommodation, transfers plus entrance fees to local attractions, Malaga Workshops, 01454 773579; www.malagaworkshops.co.uk

If you're looking for a course which offers excellent tuition and inspiring surroundings, then this informal travel writing course in stunning Andalucía, might just fit the bill. All tutors are established writers and will offer a programme of talks, tutorials and one to one sessions. Plus there will be plenty of writing time, so that you can return home a much more competent writer with hopefully a completed draft at the very least!

Travel, food and wine writing

June 1–6 2008, in St. Emilion, France, approximately £1,300,
The Writer's Workshop, 001 206 284 7121; www.thewritersworkshop.net

This specialised course will teach you the techniques of writing travel, food and wine features and even includes visits to some of the best wineries and restaurants, which are not even available to the general public.

SATW Institute for Travel Writing and Photography

January 25-27 2008, Orlando, Florida, www.satwinstitute.org

This annual intensive weekend travel writing course is aimed at amateur and professional travel writers looking to improve their writing style and who want to kick-start or step up their career.

Five good college courses:

BA Hons Magazine Journalism and Feature Writing

3 years, Southampton Solent University, 023 8031 9000, www.solent.ac.uk

This specialised course aims to nurture students into becoming brilliant feature writers and teaches them how to work to tight deadlines – which is essential for any budding magazine journalist. Students can also undertake a module on how to become a freelancer, plus they will make plenty of contacts within the industry, during the compulsory work experience placement.

BA Hons Creative Writing

Bath Spa University, 3 years, 01225 875875, www.bathspa.ac.uk

Renowned as being a top institution for creative writing, this inspiring course includes a module in travel writing whilst the other modules enable you to develop and perfect your writing and editing skills.

BA Hons Creative and Media Writing

3 years, Middlesex University, 0208 411 5555, www.mdx.ac.uk

Learn how to become a professional writer for a range of genres on this practical and inspiring course. Travel writing is also one of the modules on offer.

MA Creative and Media Writing

1 year, Swansea University, 01792 205678, www.swan.ac.uk

Hone your writing skills with the help of this year-long course, in which you will learn how to write in a range of styles as well as for different audiences. Module options include feature writing and travel writing.

Travel Writing MA

1 year, Kingston University London, 020 8547 8361, www.kingston.ac.uk

This course will really enable you to develop your skills as a travel writer and to learn all about copy-editing plus how to get your own work published. You will also study literary criticism and theory – which will help enormously when it comes to critical awareness in terms of your own writing.

Boost your writing confidence with these five CDs:

An introduction to NLP: Psychological Skills for Understanding and Influencing People

£13.99, Joseph O'Connor and Ian McDermott, Harper Thorsons Element, 0870 900 2050, www.thorsonselement.com

Neuro-Linguistic Programming has been extremely effective in changing people's attitudes and building up confidence and is becoming an increasingly popular development in applied psychology. And it might just help you to overcome your anxieties and get writing.

The 7 Habits of Highly Effective People

£10.99, Stephen R. Covey, Simon & Schuster, 020 7316 1900, www.simonsays.com

You'll soon become an effective individual yourself, thanks to what is claimed to be one of the most influential audio books ever recorded. Here, the author helps listeners to solve both personal and professional problems – so that you too can become successful in your own life.

Self Discovery

£9.99, Meditainment, 01273 325136, www.meditainment.com

Sometimes if you're stuck in a rut or suffering from writer's block, you need to take a step back and rediscover your inner self. This guided mediation audio CD helps to ease you into a state of self-discovery so that you emerge feeling revived and more self-motivated.

Total Relaxation

£9.99, Meditainment, 01273 325136, www.meditainment.com

To enter a state of inner peace and to totally recharge your batteries, then this Total Relaxation CD is the perfect antidote – you'll have restored confidence in no time.

Instant Confidence (free – as part of the book)

£10.99, Paul McKenna, Bantam Press,

With the combined help of the book and CD, Paul McKenna will be able to take you from your current situation to a place where you can fulfil your ambitions. The CD will help to improve your confidence and motivation whilst filling your mind with positive thoughts.

Ten good travel writing books:

The Art of Travel

£7.99, Alain de Botton, Penguin, www.penguin.com

This insightful guide aims to delve into the reasons as to why we as humans love to travel and along with being thought-provoking it also provides some very good pointers to bear in mind as well.

Driving Over Lemons

£6.99, Chris Stewart, Penguin Group, www.penguin.co.uk

This travel book has received a great deal of praise among both readers and critics alike and with its comical prose and vivid descriptions which literally transport you to Andalucía - it's easy to see why.

Teach Yourself Travel Writing (New Edition)

£8.99, Cynthia Dial, Hodder Education, www.teachyourself.co.uk

This user-friendly guide on how to become a travel writer is split up into easy chapters, which you can dip in and out of – making it the ideal book to have on your desk. Plus, it offers some really useful advice by a writer who obviously knows her stuff! Sections include how to sell your articles to magazines, what to do on location and even has advice on taking your own photography.

Travel Writing

£10.99, Don George, Lonely Planet Publications, www.lonelyplanet.com

Compiled by a team of successful travel writers, this is an invaluable book for anyone who is serious about becoming a professional travel writer. Learn how to write publishable travel pieces, plus how to research and pitch your ideas to magazines and newspapers.

Notes from a Small Island

£8.99, Bill Bryson, Random House, www.randomhouse.com

If you want to learn from the pros – then read a good example of travel literature. They say that in order to become a better writer, you need to read more, so this is the ideal place to start. Bill Bryson has a clever, witty writing style and in this book he travels around Britain whilst commenting on all the things he loves most about it.

The Freelance Writer's Handbook

£9.99, Andrew Crofts, Piatkus Books Ltd, 01476 541080, www.piatkus.co.uk

Including advice on travel writing, this handy book will give you inspiration on what to write and if you are already a working journalist, it will also give you ideas on finding new areas and markets for your work. Plus it also offers tips on interviewing techniques, which may come in useful during your travels.

English for Journalists

£14.99, Wynford Hicks, Routledge – Taylor & Francis Group, 020 7017 6000, www.routledge.com

Essential for journalists, this updated version covers all aspects of journalistic writing, including house-style and a glossary of terms commonly used within journalism, as well as examples of mistakes not to make. This is important for anyone who is looking to break into a career in journalism.

How to Write and Sell Travel Articles

Cathy Smith, Allison & Busby, www.allisonandbusby.ltd.uk

This popular book is a comprehensive guide for anyone who wants to become a travel writer and has been listed twice in the 'Best selling travel books' in the Independent newspaper.

Penguin Pocket Writer's Handbook

£5.99, Stephen Curtis and Martin Manser, Penguin, www.penguin.co.uk

This is the compulsory handbook for any writer in need of a quick reference for writing good and effective English. It's especially useful if you need to brush up on your spelling, grammar and punctuation.

Writing: The Hobby That Pays

£8.99, Gordon Wells, Elliot Right Way Books, 01737 832202, www.right-way.co.uk

This book teaches you the fundamental basics of writing and is a great aid for those who want to make money out of their favourite pastime. It's inspirational too.

If you enjoyed this book, you'll want Diana's book on how to write any kind of magazine article in one weekend – it will change your writing life!

By the same author

Praise for Diana Cambridge's first book

How to write for magazines... in one weekend

Canal Street Publishing Ltd
£9.99

"Your book is wonderful and so inspiring. You have definitely re-enthused me and I am now raring to go."

Review in *Bath Chronicle* February 2007

...With a track record that covers everything from writing for local newspapers to columns for nationals such as *The Guardian* and *The Times* and editing glossy magazines, Diana is in a strong position to dish out advice to aspiring writers. Indeed, she already does so, as the agony aunt for *Writers' News*. *How to write for magazines… in one weekend* is the perfect companion for someone determined to see them-selves in print… the book is full of good advice…and the wealth of experience and detail she provides makes you pretty confident that many of her disciples will be satisfied.

Dear Diana

Oh my God. I just want to say a big thank you – your book is brilliant. I ordered on 13th from Amazon and received on 14th. What a brilliant Valentines Day I had. Finished it today, bubbling with ideas and am looking forward to tackling it as a course next week when my husband is away on business. Things just bubbled up as I read.

I've had a few short stories published and a couple of articles in *The Lady* over the last couple of years and now my youngest child is older am wanting to push ahead with my writing. It is a confidence thing. I'm sure I could have done it all before but I kept talk-ing myself out of it.

Anyway, I'm ready to attack now, thanks to you and your book. What great advice you give – and so generous. I always read your pages in *Writers' News* and *Writing Magazine* (I'm a subscriber) & now I'm looking forward to putting your inspiring words into practice – I'll let you know how I get on.

A million thanks.

~ *Tracy Baines*

Dear Diana

I am writing to say a huge thank you for inspiring me to actually sit at my computer and write.

I have only just started writing after harbouring a desire to do so since I was a child. I have read so many writing self help books looking for inspiration and tips to start but have got nowhere. I just felt I would never be good enough or did not have what it takes. Your '*How to write... in one weekend*' has changed all that! I have now written several readers letters, a short story and a short opinion piece - all in 48 hours!

Many thanks for your help, I cannot rate your book highly enough.

~ *Lisa Wyatt*

Dear Diana

Your book is wonderful and so inspiring. After letting my subscription to *Writing Magazine* lapse for a year I recently renewed my membership and I am so glad I did, I would not have known about your book otherwise.

Not only have I found your articles informative but they have given me the incentive to add to the letters and articles I have had published in the past. You have definitely re-enthused me and I am now raring to go (after the ironing and prep for dinner!). Thank you again.

~ *Marianne Piesley*

Dear Diana

I have received my copy of your book this morning – thank you for your prompt response.

The weekend course is really exciting! I scan read through the introductory chapters immediately and this is the first 'how to' book that has captured my imagination so much. At present, I am nursing my husband through an illness (and I have MS but that's by the way), so I'll choose a sensible weekend and make my plans before settling down to work through the course.

~ *Shirley Davis*

Web review from *The London Writers Circle* –
**the capital's oldest and most respected circle
of writers. It has been meeting for 80 years.**

How To Write For Magazines . . . in one weekend by
Diana Cambridge, published by Canal Street Publishing Ltd. 1 Coburg Villas, Camden Road, Bath BA1 5JF.
01225 312221 www.canalstreet.org.uk £9.99

A bold claim you may think. But in the book's opening message Diana Cambridge points out that in her experience 'it's not rejection that stops talented writers seeing their work in print, it's the fact that they never get to send their work to editors.' That's the book's message. In order to do so switch off the Monday to Friday day-job with its stresses and frustrations, and embark on one well-planned writing weekend in the comfort of your own home.

I found this 164-page paperback very user friendly. Diana Cambridge is encouraging, and the arrangement of the twelve chapters, with frequent bullet points and box-outs to catch the attention, is easy to follow. 'Think DOSH' Diana advises readers considering writing for women's magazines - direct, ordinary, simple and honest. Practical matters include that all important cover letter, the do's and don'ts of submissions and, in a final chapter 'Moving On', a list of courses, how to make even one day's writing work for you, keeping fit for the task, lists of books, writing magazines, websites and conferences.

Whatever your choice this is a book full of practical tips from an experienced editor. At just under a tenner, it's good value.

~ *Monica Mukherji*

Review in *Writing* **magazine, 2007**

…Diana gives very positive and upbeat advice that will make your weekend as enjoyable as it is productive. You will be shown how and where to find ideas, how to see them from an editor's-eye viewpoint, how to craft them into copy that will meet your target magazines' needs, and how to send them out. Along the way you will acquire a new confidence and learn new skills that will keep your writing energy high and ensure that you are well motivated.

"…the perfect companion for someone who wants to see themselves in print."

"I began my 'weekend' on Wednesday evening and have now completed two articles and a letter."

Diana

I had your *How to write for magazines in one weekend* sent to me for my birthday. I will be writing a review of it as, thanks to you, I now see ideas for articles everywhere and also because you made me see success as attainable and I just can't wait!

~ *Sarah Connolly*

Dear Diana

I very much enjoyed your *How to write for magazines… in one weekend*.

Although I'm an oldie, writing for nearly 40 years now, I found much there to inspire and help me as I plod ever onwards. And yours is the first article I turn to in *Writing Magazine*. Thanks for all your expertise and understanding.

~ *Christina Green*

Hello Diana

I just wanted to let you know how much I've enjoyed doing your two-day writing course. I have done it on a Monday and Tuesday as that suited me better than the weekend. I found it a pleasure to follow and much to my surprise have completed two readers' letters and an opinion piece for *The Lady*.

If I am successful with any of this – no, when I am successful I will let you know. Your book is a great inspiration especially the motivational bits. I have enjoyed myself so much over the last two days I have booked next Monday and Tuesday in my diary for doing some more.

~ *Christobel Gardner*

Hello Diana

I just wanted to say thankyou for your book *How to write for magazines… in one weekend*. I began my "weekend" on Wednesday evening and have now completed two articles and a letter. I am just about to make a large cup of coffee and get the red pen out!

~ *Lisa McGeary*

About Canal Street Publishing Ltd

We are a small, independent publishing company dedicated to producing quality books which enhance your life, and your creative interests.

Our first two titles are

How to write magazine articles… in one weekend
(Canal Street Publishing Ltd £9.99) and

How to write travel articles… in one weekend
(Canal Street Publishing Ltd £9.99)

We believe in personal contact with our customers. We don't use call centres, or recorded messages, and we don't charge p and p – wherever you live. We're happy to take cheques. We ship all books within 48 hours.

You can visit our website at www.canalstreet.org.uk and you can also join Diana's writing club, free, at diana@canalstreet.org.uk. Just e-mail her at any time with your writing questions or comments – she replies personally to all e-mail.

We welcome new themes for our books. If you have an idea which you think would fit our list, we might be able to help. Just contact us by any route which suits you, at:

Canal Street Publishing Ltd
1 Coburg Villas
Camden Road
Bath, BA1 5JF

Or

dianacambridge@tiscali.co.uk

Or

01225 312221

So please do look us up, and let us know if you have questions, comments or ideas.

Meet our favourite freelancers

Paul Jenner

Gillian Thornton

Julie Venis

Bob Jenkins

Jos Simon

Marie Barbieri

Suzi Stembridge

John Batty

Rob Adams

Solange Hando

John Shaw

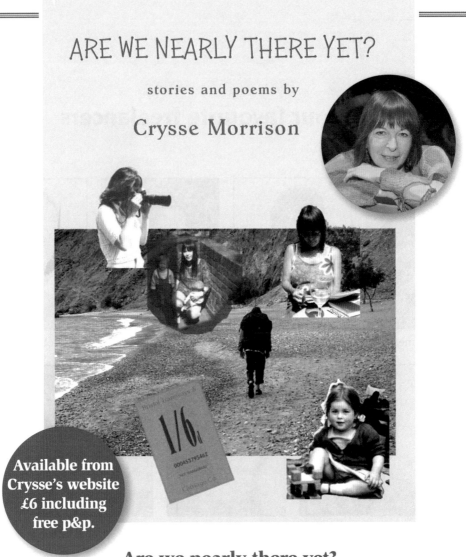

ARE WE NEARLY THERE YET?

stories and poems by

Crysse Morrison

Are we nearly there yet?

Stories and poems by writer Crysse Morrison around those universal themes of love, lust, loss, longing, and life in general. 'Most of the stories have been published or broadcast already' says Crysse 'But with the poems they seem to show a picture of the whole complexity of contemporary life. I decided to put this patchwork collection together because I'm often asked for books after my poetry performances.'

http://www.cryssemorrison.co.uk

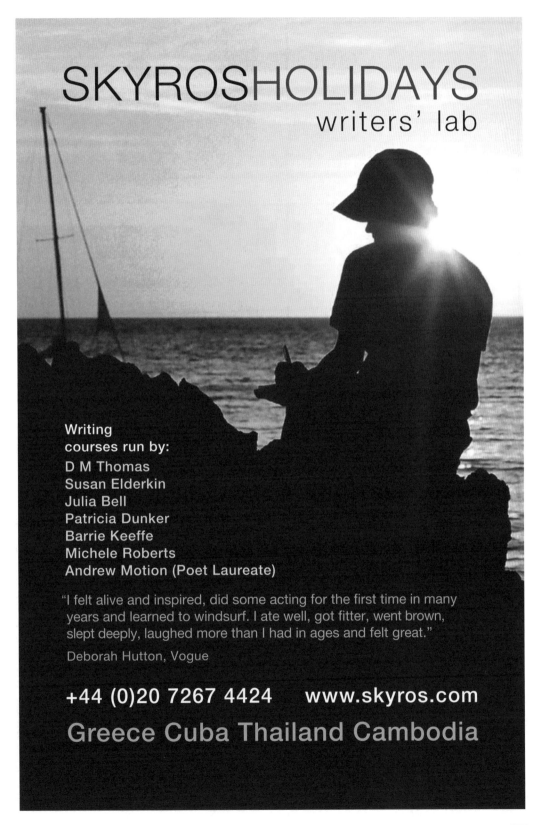

Explore your **creativity**

Mslexia tells you everything you need to know about exploring your creativity and getting into print.

No other magazine provides *Mslexia*'s unique mix of advice and inspiration; news, reviews, interviews; competitions, events, grants. All served up with a challenging selection of new poetry and prose.

Mslexia is read by top authors and absolute beginners. A quarterly masterclass in the business and psychology of writing, it's the essential magazine for women who write.

7 open submissions slots, including flash fiction, memoir and poetry

10 pages of competitions and calls for submissions

· ·

'inspired and inspiring' Sarah Waters
'manna from heaven' Rose Tremain
'diverse and brilliant' Fay Weldon
'my favourite women's magazine'
Wendy Cope

· ·

TRY BEFORE YOU BUY:
Mslexia (meat), PO Box 656, Freepost NEA5566, Newcastle upon Tyne, NE1 1BR **0191 261 6656**
diana@mslexia.demon.co.uk
www.mslexia.co.uk

· ·

Winner of the 2006 Award for Outstanding Contribution to Literature

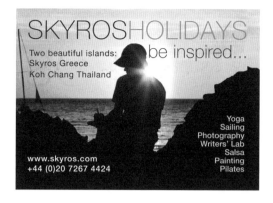

Southampton Solent University

Want to be a professional writer or journalist?

Why not join one of our dynamic degrees at Southampton Solent University and be taught by industry professionals?

All our courses are creative, many of them are distinctive, and some are unique.

BA (Hons) Journalism* (Print and Broadcast)
BA (Hons) Writing Fashion and Culture (Fashion Journalism)
BA (Hons) Magazine Journalism and Feature Writing
BA (Hons) Sport Writing
BA (Hons) Writing Popular Fiction
BA (Hons) Screenwriting

*Accredited by the NCTJ, BJTC and PTC

For further information contact Suzanne Dixon or Lisa Dibben on +44 (0)2380 319 000

Southampton Solent University
East Park Terrace
Southampton
Hampshire
SO14 0YN
Tel: +44 (0) 2380 319 000
www.solent.ac.uk

Buy that place in the sun!

**Want to write about Greece?
You'd probably love a home there.
Piraeus Bank can help**

Irini Tzortzoglou, Head of Retail Banking at Piraeus Bank, has been with the bank since the London branch was established in December 1999. She is very passionate about Greece and is happy to see that most buyers of Greek property want to live – and often to write about – their place in the Greek sun. 'This shared passion for Greece creates a stronger sense of duty to provide as good a service to our customers as possible', she says. Piraeus Bank (0845 6036 538), through its London office, aims to become a leader in providing mortgages for the purchase of property in South Eastern Europe. By combining UK standards of service with local expertise, it is able to offer a comprehensive package to its customers.